Municipal Knowledge Series

DIGITAL
CONNECTIONS

Social Media for Municipalities & Municipal Politicians

FEEDS DATA CIRCLES SEO POLITICS
MOBILE WWW SEARCH YOUTUBE ONLINE WEB CONTENT
NETWORKING TWITTER CONNECTION BLOGGER
VIDEO CONTACT BLOG WORDPRESS
RSS LINKEDIN CONNECT COMMENT LIKE FRIEND
TAG PODCAST
BUZZ COMMUNICATE GROUPS
EMAIL FOLLOWER CMS CROWDSOURCE NEWS FACEBOOK
SOCIAL MEDIA WIKIS
BOOKMARK
TUMBLR
LINKS COMMUNITY SHARE

Ian Chadwick

2012

Library and Archives Canada Cataloguing in Publication

Chadwick Ian

Digital connections: social media for municipalities and municipal politicians / Ian Chadwick.

(Municipal knowledge series)

ISBN 978-1-926843-02-5

1. Municipal government--Public relations. 2. Social media--Political aspects. 3. Communication in politics. 4. Government publicity. 5. Internet in public administration.

I. Title. II. Title: Social media for municipalities and municipal politicians. III. Series: Municipal knowledge series

JS100.C52 2012   352.7'48   C2012-902197-0

Published in Canada by
Municipal World Inc.
42860 Sparta Line
Union, Ontario N0L 2L0
2012
mwadmin@municipalworld.com
www.municipalworld.com

ITEM 0076
Municipal World — Reg. T.M. in Canada, Municipal World Inc.

The text pages of this book are printed on:

TABLE OF CONTENTS

**Dedicated with love to my wife
Susan McCallan**

Networking is not about hunting. It is about farming. It's about cultivating relationships. Don't engage in "premature solicitation." You'll be a better networker if you remember that. – *Dr. Ivan Misner, BNI*

More companies are discovering that an über-connected workplace is not just about implementing a new set of tools – it is also about embracing a cultural shift to create an open environment where employees are encouraged to share, innovate, and collaborate virtually. – *Karie Willyerd & Jeanne C. Meister, HarvardBusiness.org*

To utilize social media tools effectively and properly, you must absolutely generate spontaneous communications in direct response to what others are saying or to what is happening in that moment. Be yourself. Be conversational. Be engaged. – *Aliza Sherman, Conversify*

Quit counting fans, followers, and blog subscribers like bottle caps. Think, instead, about what you're hoping to achieve with and through the community that actually cares about what you're doing. – *Amber Naslund, Social Media Today*

A marketing person should always ask one key question when beginning to develop a social media strategy: how much chaos can this organization handle? – *Gary Stein, Ammo Marketing*

The value of being connected and transparent is so high that the roadbumps of privacy issues are much lower in actual experience than people's fears. – *Reid Hoffman, LinkedIn*

Why are we trying to measure social media like a traditional channel anyway? Social media touches every facet of business and is more an extension of good business ethics. – *Erik Qualman, author of Socialnomics*

Those who ignore the party/conversation/network when they are content and decide to drop in when they need the network may not succeed. It's pretty easy to spot those that are just joining the network purely to take – not to give. Therefore, be part of the party/conversation/network before you need anything from anyone. – *Jeremiah Owyang, web-strategist.com*

Human beings are far more likely to communicate ideas and information with others when they are emotionally engaged. Find the key issues that concern your audience and then inculcate them within your marketing plan to get an emotional response. – *Maki, doshdosh.com*

The problem with trying to determine ROI for social media is you are trying to put numeric quantities around human interactions and conversations, which are not quantifiable. – *Jason Falls, socialmediaexplorer.com*

Social media is about the people! Not about your business. Provide for the people and the people will provide for you. – *Matt Goulart, webstarcontent.com*

Most bloggers who rise above the clutter are quite often prolific – they work hard, not just writing content but networking, engaging in social media, and more. – *Darren Rowse, problogger.net*

Social media, it turns out, isn't about aggregating audiences so you can yell at them about the junk you want to sell. Social media, in fact, is a basic human need, revealed digitally online. We want to be connected, to make a difference, to matter, to be missed. We want to belong, and yes, we want to be led. – *Seth Godin, sethgodin.typepad.com*

Whether something brings them joy or pain, when people share and engage in communities, they form bonds and relationships with others who acknowledge their situation. – *Liana Evans, How to Earn Respect on Social Media, searchenginewatch.com*

Chapter 1

Opportunities & Challenges in a Networked World

Writing about social media is like writing about the weather: it changes rapidly, it's difficult to predict, today's headline is tomorrow's history lesson, and everyone has an opinion about it. By the time you read these words, it may have changed in ways I could not foresee. New tools will come out, sites will come and go, and users will find creative ways to do things that no one imagined a few years ago. Or not. That's the way of the internet.

Social networking isn't really new, and the technology that has helped it to develop has existed for decades, albeit in less sophisticated form. Social media's ancestry dates back to the first computer bulletin board systems of the late 1970s. Self-publishing, content sharing, and individual profiles were available on the internet in the late-1990s when Six Degrees came online. The first significant social networking site, Friendster, launched in 2002.

What *is* new is the rapid online proliferation of those uses and technologies we now call social networking. It's a fundamental change in the way we use the internet, from passive to interactive, monologue to dialogue, individual to collective, from a venue for technical specialists to a common platform for self-publishing.

The term "social media" refers to the tools and services that provide these networking opportunities. Social media is about: enhancing connections; a continual stream of communication and information; networks and links; sharing and shared experiences; social interactions; and fostering online communities of people who might otherwise be uncon-nected in the real world. Social media negates geographical and social barriers to allow us to connect across all boundaries.

It's also about advertising, marketing, and promotion – for yourself and your community, your events, and your activities. It has also provided new opportunities and challenges for commercial and corporate enter-prises, and the emergence of a new industry of social media marketers and consultants in the past decade.

Social media is a platform for user-generated content, a sea-change from the pre-packaged content of familiar (often commercial) websites of a few years ago. *Content Nation* is what author John Blossom calls it: the place where we all become publishers and content providers. Content can be almost anything: a comment on what you had for breakfast, a photo uploaded from your phone, a short message ("tweet") about your current activity, a link, a video, or a lengthy blog post.

Social media makes you the author, editor, and publisher. You can even create your own micro-media empire with a few tools and time, using sharing sites to host your content. The cost to start a newspaper: millions of dollars. The cost to start a blog, YouTube channel, and Facebook pro-file: pocket change.

This shift has shaken traditional media, which had a monopoly on con-tent distribution until the internet arrived. Most traditional media strug-gle to adapt to this loss of control in the new online world. The most successful have adopted social media features: reporters using Twitter, newspapers allowing open comment on their stories, etc. Some news-papers have even dropped their print editions and gone entirely online. New digital publications have not been constructed from the vertebra of traditional media, but created solely in cyberspace – many using unpaid "citizen journalists" as reporters and commentators.

It took radio 38 years to reach 50 million listeners. TV had that audience in 13 years. The world wide web did it in just seven. Facebook opened its membership to the general public in 2006 and topped 50 million mem-bers a year later. That doubled in another year. Today, Facebook has more than 800 million members. This spectacular growth is one reason social media is important.

The internet was the single largest change in communications technol-ogy since Gutenberg's movable-type press revolutionized printing, al-most 500 years ago. Mass communication has shifted from the domain of private media companies to anyone with a computer and an internet connection. Everyone online can be a publisher, editor, and broadcaster regardless of background, wealth, or training. But, only in the past decade have both the user base and the online tools matured enough to take the internet into what has since 1999 been called Web 2.0 – "participatory information sharing," collaboration, and "user-centred design." (See Appendix B for more on Web 2.0 and beyond.)

Roughly 80 percent of Canadian households have an internet connection today, according to StatsCan figures. That's about 27 million of us (from the Internet World Stats site). More than half of us access the internet through more than one device. Research firm ComScore reported in early 2011 that the average Canadian spends 43.5 hours a month online, almost twice the worldwide average of 23.1 hours. The company also noted the fastest-growing online demographic is 55-and-over users, growing by 12 percent since 2009.

Ipsos Reid pegged the time Canadians spend online a bit higher, at just over 18 hours a week for men and about 16 for women: higher than time spent watching TV. According to Ipsos Reid's Canadian Interactive Report Special Feature on Social Networking, 60 percent of Canadians online have a social networking profile. Ipsos found 86 percent of Canadians aged 18 to 34 years have a social networking profile; 62 percent of those aged 35 to 54 have profiles; and 43 percent of those 55 years and older have one. Almost all Canadians have a Facebook profile; almost 20 percent also have a Twitter account; and 14 percent are on LinkedIn.

Being connected is not only important for Canadians; it occupies a significant part of our daily life. Social networking plays a huge and growing role in our online presence.

The large number of Canadians using social media has implications for your municipal communications strategy. Provincial laws (such as Ontario's *Planning Act*) require certain notices to be published in local media. But, if more people use social media than read the local newspaper, doesn't it make sense to publish that notice on your Facebook page as well? Or, at the very least, publish a link to where that notice is stored on your municipal website? Even if it's not a requirement to do so, it's good customer service.

Municipalities will find using social media enhances your communications reach, and may engage people who haven't been engaged by municipal politics in the past – the younger voters, for example. Individual politicians may find social media also helps connect them to those same segments of the population.

The internet offers an unprecedented wealth of locations for dialogue, information dispersal, and exchange; for interactivity, sharing, and networking. Individuals and many companies took to it immediately, but governments have been slow to really embrace all the possibilities. Despite its potential, the online world is difficult to manage in ways that governments are used to managing. Even municipal governments – which are usually faster to adopt new strategies than other orders of government – find it difficult to come to grips with all the aspects, policies, resource demands, and planning required in order to dovetail the shape-shifting, free-wheeling social media environment with municipalities' existing processes and established modes of communication.

So many federal politicians and bureaucrats are already on social networks that the government released a set of guidelines for proper use of social media, in November 2011, available on the Treasury Board of Canada Secretariat website.

For municipal politicians, social media offers new opportunities to connect and interact with your electorate. It can also be a minefield, full of liabilities, legal quagmires, plus staff and resource headaches for your municipality. It can be a dangerous shoal that sinks political aspirations and careers, or it can be the place where you stake your claim as a connected, modern politician who galvanizes and engages the voters.

Like any tool, social media can be used well or poorly, actively or passively; but, because the rules are still being drafted and change frequently, many people aren't quite sure what to follow, and worry that those rules will change tomorrow.

You don't really have a choice about whether or not to use social media – just a decision about when to start and how much effort to put into it. Social networking is here to stay and getting more integrated with our daily lives.

In this book, I outline some of the benefits and risks of using social media, both for your municipality and for yourself. Some of it – like security and confidentiality – should be common sense for computer users by now, but being online seems to make some of us forget our public persona is present, not just our private face.

I will also make the case for developing a separate social media section within your municipal communications policy, if you don't already have one. At the very least, you should have a written municipal communications policy, but I strongly encourage you to develop something more comprehensive for social media and online activity.

Chapter 2

The Whole World is Watching

The numbers are staggering. By the end of 2010, there were almost 267 million websites with more than 10 billion individual pages; more than 21 million websites were added in 2010 alone; 152 million blogs were online; 25 billion tweets were sent by 180 million Twitter users. That year, 600 million Facebook users shared 30 billion pieces of content (links, notes, photos, etc.); two billion videos were watched every day on YouTube; and two billion internet users worldwide sent 107 trillion emails – an average of 294 billion messages per day.

Like stars in the galaxy or grains of sand on a beach, the immensity of the internet is impossible to comprehend. You cannot connect with even a respectable percentage of all the sites, videos, blogs, messages, email messages, tweets, photos, e-books, and other content. When you couple those numbers with statistics that show 71 percent of tweets sent on Twitter receive no response and are not re-tweeted, and that 89 percent of all email is spam (roughly 262 billion items per day), you feel like a small child staring into the night sky wondering at its vastness and distance, and feeling very alone.

So, you might be forgiven if you assumed that what you posted, wrote in a blog, or shared in a risky photo on Facebook might get overlooked in the deluge of data and content that exists online. After all, you're just one in two billion users, your photo was just one of 30 billion items on Facebook. You have better odds of winning the lottery than being tagged online. Right?

Wrong.

In fact, the whole world *is* watching and, with rare exception, everything you put online is public and accessible to everyone else. Just because you don't get responses doesn't mean you are being ignored.

Archive of Online Activity

Most of the internet gets archived in some form or another: what you post or display could be available for others to find for a very long time. I looked at the Internet Archive Wayback Machine in late 2011 and found pages I built in early 1997, stored for anyone to critique. Pretty embarrassing design, but at least the content is innocuous enough to spare me more than minor embarrassment.

Others are not so fortunate. In early 2011, New York Congress Representative Anthony Weiner sent inappropriate photographs of his underwear-clad crotch via his Twitter account to a 21-year-old female college student. Very soon, it was national news. Weiner initially tried to deny the allegations, claiming his Twitter account had been hacked. But, as more images and allegations of similar behaviour became public, Weiner admitted his "prank," and to having had several electronic relationships with women over the past three years. His denials and those photos will be online for many, many more years.

Inappropriate tweets can even cause international conflict. In the fall of 2011, Linda Sobeh Ali, the Palestinian envoy to Canada, was told by the foreign affairs department she was no longer welcome in Ottawa after she tweeted a link to a video that the federal government deemed "an offensive diatribe against Jews." After her tweet, the Canadian government formally protested to the Palestinian Authority and requested her replacement. A spokesperson for Foreign Affairs Minister John Baird called her tweet a "serious lack of judgment." Ms. Sobeh Ali closed her Twitter account after the ruckus.

It's another lesson that every eye is on you, and that other users are quick to find out when you've strayed from your public responsibilities into your private persona – especially when that private persona acts like a hormonally-charged adolescent. Nothing you ever say or do online is truly confidential or forgotten. Author Mitch Joel calls this the "long tail of content."

This is equally true of municipal email. Your email is archived somewhere. Municipal servers keep it for years, maybe decades. It is part of the public process. Anyone can file a freedom of information request to get it and, aside from some topics that are legitimately confidential under in-camera legislation (e.g., personnel issues), all of it can be made public – even those jokes of dubious taste you shared with another councillor!

Once you take office, you lose much of the right to privacy that an un-elected citizen has. You are a public figure, a role you play 24 hours a day while you hold office. Everything you do or say is open to criticism, publication, and analysis. You cannot shift to a private persona and make insults online; nor can you post inappropriate photographs, and then dis-tance your public persona from them. No one will see the difference. The public will perceive everything you do and write online as an act of their elected representative.

Unexpected Exposure

What you put online gets spread around the web in unexpected ways. What you post on Facebook may get copied to sites like Lamebook and Failbook (parody sites that present the worst of Facebook's entries). It may be picked up by news sites and blogs. Even if you manage some damage control on Facebook, your legacy may linger elsewhere.

Companies do background checks on potential employees, searching so-cial media for indications of behaviour, attitude, and activity. Some em-ployers monitor Facebook and Twitter to see if an employee has posted anything unflattering or critical – comments and photographs posted on social networks have been cause for dismissal. Conversely, applicants search the social networks for comments from and about their potential future employers.

The internet creates a sense of community and intimacy with our online correspondents. Social media heightens that sensation through terms like friends, communities, circles, and groups, used to describe online ac-quaintances, many of whom may be total strangers to you. Of about 250 "friends" in my Facebook account, and those following me on Twitter, I have met only about a quarter of them. Will my many online friends and followers honour my confidence if I post something indiscreet and pot-entially harmful to my career? Not likely.

Treat your online presence as if you are on stage in front of a large audi-ence, rather than in the company of a few intimate friends. Don't treat it like a private activity you practice alone in your home, and you'll be less likely to put anything foolish or damaging online.

Remember: the whole world *is* watching.

Chapter 3

Civil Debate and Other Lost Causes

The internet is not to blame for the demise of civil debate and polite discussion. Civility has declined for decades, long before the internet came into being. The devolution is due, in part, to the society-shaking collision of popular culture, mass media, technology, political posturing, and the automobile, all within a very short time.

Yes, the family car. As Stephen Carter points out in his book *Civility: Manners, Morals and the Etiquette of Democracy*, the automobile created the illusion that we travel alone. While public transit requires people to follow at least basic rules of social interaction and crowd behaviour, cars isolate us from the others on the road; we behave as if the road was our private property, and all others on it trespassers.

Similarly, the internet encourages us to believe we are alone and not among thousands, even millions of simultaneous users. Being online from home on a private computer encourages this sense of solitude. We can sit at home in our pajamas and surf the world as if it's our private playground, a place where we make all the rules.

We often behave online as if no one else is reading what we post, as if it is a private diary and we can post anything we please without fear of it being found. We vent and spume. We call names, we insult colleagues and co-workers. We react angrily to challenges, criticism, and opposition, fighting back against interlopers of a different political stripe. We write nasty replies to other posters, and slag one another over perceived slights. Online posts often drip with venom, anger, and vituperation. Un-civil comment and debate has become the norm online.

New Empowerment

Thanks to social media, we are all empowered to comment on the world's events in ways never before available. No need to pen a lengthy letter to the editor or wait on hold in a phone queue to comment to a talk-show host. Just type a few words into a comment box and your words are available for the whole world to share. Everyone's opinion has a place to shine.

In late 2011, as rebel forces closed in on the late Libyan dictator Muammar Gaddafi's stronghold of Sirte, a family photo album un-covered in one of his mansions was scanned and posted online. The images show a rather ordinary, even banal, family amidst a kitschy lifestyle: a proud but rumpled father holds his new baby; the family out for an afternoon stroll; a son happily learning to ride a horse; wife and children posed on a couch by a TV set.

Many of these comments below, taken intact from the Daily Mail On-line's website that reported the story, say more about the posters them-selves than about Gaddafi:

➤ I'm getting Tired of writing bout this Monster..I just want him and his Evil Family..DEAD. Asap!

➤ What a poor misunderstood evil despot. If only Nero were alive they could commiserate in each other's sorrows as like-minded kin.

➤ What an ugly, tasteless Addams Family bunch of chavs!

➤ This hideous looking family should be put on world tour as a cir-cus. Use the money gained toward rebuilding Libya.

➤ What a pity NATO missiles missed killing him, Gaddafi I mean.

➤ One word describes the lot of them, SCUM!

➤ That's not his wife Safiya – that's Gaddafi in drag.

None of these inane, spiteful comments came from the rebels, or any other Libyans. None came from residents of nearby North African or Middle Eastern countries. They all came from residents of Britain, France, Canada, South Korea, and the U.S. who felt it was their right to comment, even though none of them had any direct relationship with either Libya or Gaddafi.

Similar comments are posted online in the thousands every day: angry, violent, intolerant, insulting, full of invective, and usually poorly written.

Attracting the Trolls

The ease of making a comment also leads people to respond before really considering the consequences. Even innocuous posts can draw nasty responses. A Facebook link to a news item about the discovery of Earth-like extra-solar planets heated up after one person posted: *"were the thirds planet because it revolves around the sun and its a hint to the holy trinity fact. An a big bang in space would expand not come together simple common sense no gravity see any bang on earth would do the same. explosions do not create they decimate. fact.* [sic]*"* This thread quickly became a virulent science-versus-religion debate, rather than a discussion about the discovery itself.

People who post online solely to invite reaction and start arguments are called "trolls." A basic rule for social media use is: never engage a troll in debate. You can't win; you can only make yourself look intolerant, angry, or foolish – or all three. And then, you'll have the embarrassment of seeing your responses re-posted on other sites to spread your embarrassment around.

It's difficult to express a wide and deep range of emotions in text alone. Skilled authors can do it, of course. That's why we have great literature. But, most people online are not skilled writers. Many use platforms like Twitter that compress responses down to a minimum number of characters, or post through awkward cell phones or tablets that encourage brevity over comprehension. The potential for misunderstanding is greatly increased by these tools.

To be fair, negative, poorly-worded, and inane comments get a lot more attention than the many positive, thoughtful, intelligent, and well-written ones. You have to deal with both, and cannot block the bad and simply accept the good. That's not how the internet works. What municipal politicians and staff must learn is how to deal efficiently and calmly with the negative posters, without taking the comments personally.

Practising the Principles of Civility

Civil debate on the internet is not necessarily dead, but – like proper grammar online – it may be on its deathbed. The only way to keep it alive is to practise the principles of civility: be polite and formal with strangers, don't respond with anger, don't insult or call names, respect differences of opinion, and think about your response first. As a politician, this should be foremost in your mind, because your circumstances are different from those of most posters.

You will likely be posting under your own name. Because of the levels of anonymity that many social sites allow, you may find yourself shadow-boxing with unknown or even anonymous posters when you get into an online debate. You won't know if they are adults, male or female, residents of your municipality, or even residents of Canada. Sometimes, you won't even know if what appears to be multiple posters is really just one angry person posting under different identities (some blogs and forums allow anonymous comments, while others allow you to create a different username with every post).

As a politician, you won't be able to engage in civil exchanges with everyone because others can (and will at times) use invective, insult, rant, and make personal attacks while you keep a polite public persona, or risk damage to your reputation. Keep to the high ground and remain civil despite the flailing and groaning around you. Say please, thank you, and be respectful. After the ranting, your attacker may even engage in real debate – once he or she has gotten through the anger.

And, my advice to all politicians is this: grow a thicker skin.

As blogger Erin Bury wrote, "Don't say anything online that you wouldn't want plastered on a billboard with your face on it."

Chapter 4

What Social Media Isn't

Being today's hot topic doesn't mean social media is the answer to your problems. Hype about "how great social media is" will often be presented by people or companies looking to make money from teaching you how to take advantage of it. People who have invested heavily in social media are quick to laud it and defend their investment, but does it really live up to the praise heaped on it? For all its potential, social media isn't always what it's cracked up to be.

Recognize the Limitations

Social media isn't a builder. It's just a set of tools, and not any one tool in particular. Tools alone don't fix anything. They need builders, architects, workers, and a plan to make them useful. You must take an active, leading, and conscientious role to make sure you use social media effectively and appropriately.

Social media won't fix your problems or create solutions any more than a hammer and a box of nails will fix a housing shortage. Like any tool, it can be used well, or used poorly. Whoever wields that tool will make it a success or a failure. If you want to build an online community and engage your municipality online, you will have to do the work yourself. Social media won't do it for you.

Social media won't save or resurrect your political career, especially if you've made a mess out of it. People may forget a newspaper or TV story that was harmful to your career in a month or two; but, online, it can circulate and grow for years. A *faux pas* on social media may haunt you for a long time because it can be shared, retweeted, and reposted on other sites.

Social media won't make your municipality into a wonder of the world or blossom into an overnight economic success. Social media *is* another way to promote and market your municipality; but, that alone won't convince people to move there. You need something solid behind the online lures to get their interest, and a lot of backup material and programs to convince them. Businesses will not make relocation decisions based solely on your Facebook page; however, they may use social media to make initial connections.

Social media won't turn your polarized electorate into a community. It won't turn your opponents into supporters or solve your staffing issues. However, if you are diligent and constant about using it, social media can connect you and your municipality to the world in new and exciting ways, and provide additional opportunities for interaction and engagement. It can help you engage your opponents in the discussion.

Social media isn't the solution to all the trials and tribulations municipalities and their politicians face. In fact, it can make many of them worse by bringing the public into the decision-making process at the wrong time. A lot of conflicting voices can make the options muddier. The loudest voice may get the most attention.

Social media can be a part of the answer you seek – if you need public interaction, engagement, and communications in your solution. Use it as part of the existing process, not as an alternative to it.

Social media isn't a friendly, cohesive, online community of like-minded people sharing common goals. It's millions of individuals connected through the particular tool you're currently using, some of whom may share your interests, goals, beliefs, or ideals ... but many will not. It's democracy without borders, barriers, or restrictions. It is sometimes loud and noisy, and often very active. Be prepared for challenges, resistance, and confrontation; manage them wisely and calmly.

Negative opinions aren't necessarily bad; they can be an opportunity to present your position in a more positive light and explain yourself more fully. Getting no response may be worse than getting a negative one; because, in silence, you have no way of gauging how the audience is reacting. When you get a negative comment, don't ignore it, but engage the author – in a polite, respectful manner.

Social media isn't a haven of irritable teens and 20-somethings with a grudge against society, all of whom express their angst with bad grammar and worse spelling, while they comment about what they had for breakfast. It only *seems* that way at times. In fact, the 50-plus users are the fastest-growing demographic of social media today, and conversations can be wide-ranging and intelligent. And, sometimes, they can be about a choice of breakfast cereal.

Social media is not a structured environment for linear dialogue or academic debate. It's not a place for a one-on-one discussion about issues; it's a noisy, rambunctious democracy with everyone clamouring to be heard at once. On some sites – forums and newsgroups – discussion may be controlled and comments moderated; but, on the popular sites like Facebook, it's a free-for-all. That doesn't mean it's not constructive, just not as structured as you may be used to.

Social media isn't a classroom. Chaos thrives online and everyone has the same level of empowerment to comment. If a post is truly offensive, you can complain. But, use the complaint system wisely – and infrequently. Spurious complaints over comments may be construed as whining over appropriate opposition, or even against freedom of expression. These will win you no more than scorn from the system administrators.

Social media may not be the best tool for marketing, advertising, and promoting. Many users simply ignore the obvious attempts at promotion and focus on their conversations and comments instead. Tired of aggressive marketing streams, they "unlike" corporate or municipal pages to cut the feed down to a more manageable stream. You're competing for attention with many commercial and public enterprises. Before you simply dive in, map a strategy for promotion across more than one platform.

Social media isn't the magic wand or silver bullet to fix bad customer service, poor relations with stakeholders, bad products, or poor planning. Fix those problems before you go online with the results. Otherwise, you're just marketing your problems. Use social media to make your successes work for you. If you have someone dedicated to monitoring it and responding when issues arise, social media can provide more immediate response to problems or questions. If you monitor it sporadically or infrequently, you will only compound poor customer relations.

Social media isn't a monologue. It has to be a dialogue, and not just with one or two users – with everyone. Democracy is not measured by how it achieves consensus, but rather by how it manages dissent. You need to listen to all the voices, not just the ones that agree with you.

Social media isn't a short-term fix. It isn't something you can do once and ignore. It's not an easy or painless solution, either. Social networks are like gardens: they require a long-term commitment and constant monitoring. Because the social media players may change, you should pay attention to how the technology and the platform trends develop, so you can be prepared to shift your focus and efforts if necessary. Visiting sites like <mashable.com>, <socialmedia.org>, <socialmediatoday.com>, or <smartblogs.com> regularly will help keep you informed. Your IT people can suggest others, or help you stay abreast of the technology.

Social media isn't your private soapbox. It's *everybody's* soapbox and everyone using it feels he or she has not only the right to an opinion, but that his or her opinion carries equal weight to yours. Expect challenges, criticism, even insults and attacks, as well as support and accolades. Or, sometimes, you'll simply be ignored, which may be worse than attracting criticism. If you use social media as a vehicle to simply keep people informed and up to date, then that silence may be appropriate. But, social media works best when it involves conversation, not just declaration.

Social media isn't the right place to post your personal gripes against colleagues, co-workers, bosses, peers, family, teachers, fellow council members, or anyone else you feel isn't giving you the respect you deserve. As a public figure, your comments on social media carry the same impact as if you put them in a letter to the local newspaper, possibly with even greater readership. Issues are fair game for comment, but don't criticize others on social media or make personal attacks.

Just because it's a global community doesn't mean the rest of the world will pay attention to you. A potential worldwide audience doesn't mean it's an *actual* audience. The vastness of the available content and the constant uploading of new content make it difficult for any particular piece to stand out globally. You're more likely to get a response from your local audience if your content has something relevant, useful, entertaining, or important to say to outsiders. As former U.S. Speaker of the House Tip O'Neill famously said, "All politics is local."

Social Media Is Here to Stay

Social media didn't succeed because of its whizz-bang technology. It succeeded because it met some basic human needs: to communicate, congregate, and share. The technology only facilitated fulfilment of these needs. Hundreds of millions of users feel the urge to say something to others and the platforms gave them a place to say it.

Social media isn't just Facebook. While Facebook is certainly the biggest player in the social media spectrum at the moment, and has led the way in creating certain styles of social networking, it isn't the only player. Other platforms and sites compete to become the "next big thing." Other sites may offer a better service or community, including many location-based niche services, like <foursquare.com>. Even "anti-Facebook" social networking sites like <unthink.com> attempt to offer alternate models of use.

Look at the whole array of sites and platforms to appreciate how widespread social networking has become, and what special or unique service each site offers. Choose those that best serve your expectations and goals, but don't over-extend yourself. Just don't neglect Facebook in favour of a lot of smaller sites.

Social media isn't fixed in the firmament of the internet. It's an ever-changing environment where ideas and implementations rise and fall according to how well consumers take to them. Social media sites often change. Facebook has reinvented itself several times, as have others. Some older players have left the field; some new ones have entered. But, while the platforms have evolved, and the audience shifted loyalties to the newer platforms, the basic concepts behind social networking – collaboration and connectivity – remain the same. Stay informed about the trends and be prepared to shift your platform as necessary.

Social media isn't going away. It isn't a fad; it isn't a novelty like chia pets, hula hoops, and pet rocks. It may be transformed, it may evolve, it may go through many gyrations as it grows. But, it's here for the long term. It's too important – and too heavily used – to ignore. Use it.

Chapter 5

Who's on First?
The Major Players

While social networking takes in many of today's internet platforms – including forums, blogs, retail sites, photo and video sharing sites, and newsgroups – a small group of popular sites dominate today's social media. These sites have managed to find the right blend of usability and ease, while offering a sense of shared experience and belonging to its users.

Some argue that an online community is a pseudo-community, a simulacrum; but, for most users, it's a real community. People feel protective of their online community and supported by it, even if it doesn't provide everything tangible a physical community can offer. Social media groups act as neighbourhoods, or micro-communities, not just as global connections.

According to a Nielsen report from late 2011, social media and blogs are used by 80 percent of the internet users in the U.S., and take up most of their online time (about 23 percent, more time than Americans spend on games, email, and searching combined). Insites Consulting estimated that 73 percent of European users and more than 70 percent of internet users worldwide access social networks.

Ipsos Reid says 86 percent of all Canadian social networkers have a social networking profile with Facebook. Canadian social networking use grew from about 21 million unique visits in 2009 to 24 million in 2010. Canadian blog visits grew from 16 million to almost 18 million in that same time.

Many popular sites online are not classified as "social media" – Google, Amazon, Wikipedia, and eBay are among the most frequently visited. However, these and other sites have aspects of social networking. For example, you can review or rate products on many online retail sites; you can also comment on news stories on media sites and on wikis. Other sites offer social ways to share and rate media such as videos and photos. There are even socially-interactive games.

Conversational Media Sites

The focus in this chapter is on the sites that are specifically designed for social interaction. These "conversational media" sites are designed to encourage dialogue and interaction between users. Of the 15 most popular websites (in English), according to Alexa's ranking in October 2011, five are among the social media sites listed below in this chapter. Most of the rest have some sort of social networking capability.

It is very important to keep two things in mind when developing your social media strategy. First, all of these platforms are primarily commercial enterprises. Even if the service to you is free, their ultimate goal is to make money. They do so through a combination of advertising, products sales, and commissions, as well as "rental" fees for space or traffic. Your profile and your connections with friends provide a lot of detailed information for targeted marketing. Some sites may even sell user information to other companies, although not the larger sites.

The second thing to remember is that *their* rules define the game; your rules don't. These sites can decide arbitrarily what is allowed, what gets shared, who can use the service, and what can be posted. And, those rules can change anytime. Any of these sites can change what they offer as features, their layout, and their services without warning.

In later chapters, I'll explain how and when to use these services.

Facebook

At the top of the list is Facebook, the elephant in the room. With more than 800 million users (Q3 2011), Facebook is the world's largest social networking site and shows no sign of slowing its growth. It has as many subscribers today as there were total internet users in 2004. If Facebook were a country, it would be the world's third largest. Its relevance cannot be overstated.

Nielsen's 2011 survey showed Americans collectively spend a total 53.5 billion minutes a month on Facebook. In early 2011, Google reported that Facebook had reached one trillion monthly page views (another analytics company disputed that figure, reporting 467 billion – still a staggeringly huge amount). Almost all Canadians with a social media profile have a Facebook profile.

Facebook is the most popular social site for Canadians: more than 20 million visits in 2010, double the number of Canadian visitors to second-place Blogger. When you consider Facebook had 140 million worldwide visitors in May 2011 alone, you get a picture of how popular it is.

The average Facebook session lasts 37 minutes: reading posts, commenting, checking pages, and looking at messages. That's roughly half the time the typical user spends reading a Sunday newspaper, and longer than many people spend on weekday papers, according to an NRS survey. That's just Facebook – most users have at least one more social media account and spend additional time on it.

One of the reasons for Facebook's popularity is its all-in-one feel. It's the "Swiss Army knife" of social media sites. You can comment, respond, like, share, post videos and links, upload photos, join groups, create polls, and even play games without ever leaving Facebook. True, it's not as good at some specific functions as focused sites like Flickr or Wordpress; but, it does everything reasonably well without forcing the user to leave the site.

Facebook also makes it easy to connect with other people. In a Nielsen survey from late 2011, 89 percent of all social media users found or maintained contact with old friends, 88 percent did the same for family contacts, and 70 percent found new friends through the site. Connectivity is crucial for Facebook users.

Facebook recently announced an elegant and simple video-conferencing feature will be added, a reaction to the video conferencing built into Google+. And then, Facebook announced a new page type aimed at job seekers and employers, a "social jobs partnership" with several U.S. agencies intended to help the struggling American economy create an employment resource.

Facebook itself is a job creator. In September 2011, the University of Maryland issued a report saying Facebook has created more than 235,000 jobs and contributed $15.7 billion to the U.S. economy. A healthy micro-industry of developers who work on Facebook apps and page designs has emerged.

Basically, Facebook wants to be for social media what Wikipedia is for human knowledge: the single go-to site everyone visits. And, as they add features and services, they move towards that goal.

Because of its popularity and growing user base, many politicians and municipalities have created Facebook pages that combine interaction with self-promotion. Some municipalities have multiple Facebook pages for different departments, activities, events, etc.

The advantage of Facebook is access to a potentially huge market. But, Facebook requires you to use its "friends" system to connect with others, or to purchase ads to find those "friends." You must work at it a bit to get yourself befriended or liked. You will not be able to see all of the information about individuals or groups unless you make that connection.

While you can spend money and resources customizing your Facebook pages, the core attraction is that the basic stuff is free. The familiarity of the standard design helps users recognize a Facebook page, and tinkering with it too much may confuse or turn away some users who cannot find expected content areas. However, you may want to look into ways to optimize your page to help promote your particular branding.

Facebook is suitable for both organizations and individuals. It's generally a conversation service, with short comments and exchanges between users.

A Facebook page and a Facebook profile are not the same thing; and a Facebook group is different again. Individuals can have friends, pages have fans ("likes"), and groups have members.

You can open a business account, and create linked pages, but you cannot have a personal account *and* a business account at the same time. See Chapter 12 for a fuller discussion.

While individuals need their own profile ("wall"), and may only need that profile, any organization will also need its own page or pages. Facebook only allows one profile to be associated with any page, even if you have multiple pages, and it must be set up by a person. That means someone within your organization will have to take on this responsibility and create a profile that can be associated with those pages. More on this in Chapter 12.

YouTube

YouTube is the world's biggest video-sharing site and the second-largest search engine, next to Google. It began in late 2005 and, by the end of 2010, more than three billion YouTube videos were being watched every day. More than 13 million hours of video were uploaded to YouTube that year alone, about seven hours per minute. More than 100 million views every day come from mobile users, roughly five percent of YouTube viewers, and growing rapidly.

YouTube's success lies, in part, in making it easy for users to link to or embed videos on their own sites. Seventeen million YouTube accounts are connected to at least one other social media service. YouTube has also streamlined the uploading process, and many programs now offer simple, built-in uploading to the site.

Since YouTube hosts the video, the linking site isn't using its own storage and has less bandwidth demand on its servers than when hosted locally. That has made YouTube attractive for many municipalities, individuals, and companies.

Quality has also increased as the service developed. Starting with a low 320 x 240 pixel resolution, YouTube now supports full HD video, and even has 3D support. It has gone from a site for home videos to being a repository of professional and commercial products as well.

I recently purchased an off-the-shelf dental care product that advertised "As seen on YouTube" on its package – an indication of how much YouTube has supplanted television in competition for the viewing audience. The product also claimed "4.5 out of 5 stars" from Facebook fans.

It is now essential to any music career to post your or your band's music videos on YouTube. TV stations and movie houses post previews of upcoming shows on YouTube, too.

YouTube not only hosts videos, but allows viewers to subscribe, rate, and comment on them, thus creating a platform for interaction and community. Analytics allows account holders to see how many views they get, where viewers are located, and even get a demographic breakdown.

YouTube has provided the "citizen journalist" with an important visual platform. Since anyone with a digital camera or smartphone can record video and upload it easily, YouTube has become a prime source for news and information content, often breaking news long before traditional media can do so. Look at the videos that emerged almost immediately following the capture and death of Libyan leader Muammar Gaddafi: almost all of them were recorded on the smartphones of his rebel captors and uploaded within minutes.

For municipalities, YouTube is a good platform for "lure" videos, special event promotions, council meetings, even video advertisements for jobs. Downtowns use YouTube to promote local shopping, or a farmers' market. It is also used by consumer groups to advocate for local issues and initiatives.

For politicians, YouTube can be used for webcasts (aka video podcasts) with opinions, events in which you had a role, election campaigns, and monologues. Millions of people make videos of themselves – commenting on social, political, religious, and even personal matters – and post them to YouTube. Viewers will feel free to comment and argue, so it is important to accept the two-way nature of YouTube. If you have sufficient content, you can also develop a channel that hosts your own videos only, to get the most recognition.

Because users sometimes record copyrighted TV or movie clips and post them online, YouTube has faced several challenges over copyright infringement, and has been forced to remove contested content several times. Anything you post should not violate copyright laws. That includes any music you select as a background or soundtrack.

YouTube has also made a strenuous effort to block racist and pornographic videos from being uploaded to its site. Its user community generally seems to approve of this censorship.

Blogger, Wordpress, Typepad, and Tumblr

I lump these and other blogging sites together. They provide a free platform for users to create and publish blogs – digital diaries, reviews, comments, analysis, and opinion. Some offer additional features and premium services through a paid subscription.

Blogs have no set styles or content: they can be whatever you want. You can create your blog and start writing within minutes of opening an account.

Wordpress has the advantage of offering a free, stand-alone package that can be run on your own server using their software (and can even be used to create non-blog websites). They and the rest of these companies host free blogs on their own servers. For most users, hosted services are sufficient, unless you need a URL that has your own website name in it, not the name of the service provider (i.e., <myblog.wordpress.com>).

Blog sites have evolved from simple electronic diaries ("web logs") to social media platforms by adding features like feedback or comments; "like," "share," and "follow" buttons; RSS feeds; ratings; associated photo galleries and video presentations; polls; and links to Facebook, Twitter, and other social media sites. Blogs can also be cooperative, written by teams of users, not just an individual.

While individuals can use blogs to make personal comment and statements, municipalities can use blogs to present a wide variety of ongoing topics, from recreational strategies to planning issues.

According to Blogpulse, there were almost 174 million blogs by Q3, 2011, with 900,000 blog posts made every day. While bloggers have gained considerable credibility as opinion makers and commentators in the political realm, the sheer number means you must have something important to say to get noticed. Local blogs may not have a large readership, but they will probably have a dedicated core audience because the topics will be relevant to your immediate community.

Tumblr is often described as a micro-blogging platform. Like Twitter, it encourages brevity in posts, although Tumblr is more flexible in what content it allows than most of its micro-blogging competition.

Blogs are hard work. They require a lot of writing, and that takes time. To keep your audience, you need to keep your blog current and write frequently. Nothing kills a blog audience faster than an old, stale post with no new updates. More on blogging in Chapter 11.

Twitter

Twitter is like a telegraph system: short comments only. The maximum number of characters you can put into a "tweet" is 140, or roughly 20 words. Along with text messaging on cellphones, this restriction has encouraged the development of a shorthand writing style that can baffle newcomers: CUL8R, BRB, IMHO, LOL, TLDR, OMG, and LMAO.

"Are 140 characters enough to make or break a federal election campaign?" asked Bill Curry, *Globe & Mail* reporter, on March 27, 2011. Curry described the spring 2011 federal election as "Canada's first social media election."

"The defeat of the Conservative government unleashed a torrent of political tweets," Curry noted. "By midafternoon Sunday, more than 14,000 tweets had been sent out during the first day-and-a-half of the campaign related to the election or Canadian politics. With a potential reach of more than 16 million people, it was a dramatic spike from the less than 2,000 tweets on the same topics the weekend before," he wrote.

Others have called Twitter a "virtual watercooler," an online place where people meet to chat casually about nothing in particular. Interesting tweets get "retweeted" like office gossip. Retweeting can be a measure of the author's influence or popularity.

The strength of Twitter lies in being able to tweet through any tablet, laptop, or smartphone, so users can tweet almost anywhere. The immediacy of Twitter allows it to be used like an instant messaging service, too: tweets get posted as soon as they are sent. Twitter users posted 3,283 tweets per second following the 2010 World Cup soccer match between Japan and Denmark. In 2011, Twitter boasted 200 million tweets and more than 1.6 billion searches a day.

Because Twitter can be very cluttered when you follow a lot of people, users can arrange tweets in lists to create more manageable displays. Twitter is also enhanced by numerous external applications (apps) that extend the power of its basic service. Twitterfeed, for example, feeds content from your blog back to Twitter (and to Facebook). TwiHaiku is for posting brief poems.

The average Twitter session is 23 minutes. Upper-tier political parties have software to track tweets, watching for mentions, trends, and reactions. During campaigns, this is critical knowledge for strategists.

Many Twitter users put links into tweets to direct readers to more content on another site. Tweets then become shorthand connections to other sites. Many celebrities also use Twitter to connect with their fan base. Lady Gaga, Justin Bieber, and Britney Spears, for example, each have more Twitter followers than the entire populations of Sweden, Israel, Greece, Chile, or Australia. However, Twitter has often been used for hoaxes, to misdirect or confuse authorities, and to simply cause trouble, too.

"Once people were yelling 'fire' in a crowded theatre. Now the whole world is like the crowded theatre," said Ryan Calo, a researcher at the Stanford Center for Internet and Society in a CNN interview. "It's so easy just to sort of shoot out a line on Twitter about something. There's a real lowering of inhibitions."

Twitter has recently announced integration with Apple's iOS, which will make it an integral component with iPads and iPhones. This will greatly strengthen Twitter's position as a social networking tool. Twitter apps are also available as add-on apps for most smartphones.

Unlike some social networking sites, you don't need an account to see a Twitter user's tweets or to search for keywords in tweets, if the tweets are marked public. You *will* need an account, however, to follow the sender or to see their profile information.

You need to know how to use two basic Twitter features: hashtags ("#") for identifying searchable keywords within a tweet (such as #municipal or #ukulele); and "@" for identifying users by name (i.e., @iwchadwick is mine). Sites like <hashtags.org> can track trends in Twitter by searching for words identified by hashtags in tweets. Check <politwitter.ca> for a list of Canadian politicians who tweet.

Twitter doesn't have a lot of serious competition for its niche. Plurk is ranked around 1,300th worldwide. An earlier competitor, Pownce, closed in 2008.

LinkedIn

Sometimes described as "Facebook without the chatter," LinkedIn is a business-related social networking site aimed at professionals and companies, with more than 120 million members, including representatives from all of the Fortune 500 companies. It's often used by municipal administration and staff for networking because of its "gated-access" approach that keeps content from being viewed by people outside the approved group of contacts.

LinkedIn is described as social networking with people you know (and Facebook as social networking with people you used to know). It's generally quieter, and posts have more relevant content. Users can follow companies on LinkedIn, and get notifications of job offers from them. Municipalities can post jobs there, too.

LinkedIn allows you to make your profile available to Google's search engine, which can heighten your visibility online. It has a reference check tool that companies and municipalities can use in their hiring process.

Nielsen's poll from September 2011 showed 48 percent of people use social networking sites for business contacts, and 28 percent to look for a job. LinkedIn offers a resume-style profile that can be used when job hunting or making connections, so it can be used to advertise jobs and search for potential candidates, too.

Facebook has launched its own app for professionals, called "Branch-Out," and Google+ launched its business pages in late 2011.

Google+ and MySpace

One is on the way up, the other on the way down, respectively.

Launched in 2003, MySpace reigned as the most popular social networking site until Facebook overtook it in 2008. In 2006, MySpace was the most visited website in the U.S., surpassing even Google, and boasted 1,600 workers. In late 2011, it was ranked number 103 in traffic, and had reduced its workforce to around 200. The company sold to Rupert Murdoch for $580 million in 2005 – valued at $12 billion in 2008 – and was resold in 2011 for a mere $35 million.

MySpace's failure to compete is the source of much palaver online. Some say it was too ad-dense, or it began as a file sharing and website hosting service that stumbled into social networking, but was unable to remake itself as fully or as rapidly as Facebook to meet consumer demands. Commentators have written MySpace was reactive, not innovative; it had problems with spammers, sexual predators, and porn; its design was tired; its organization was chaotic; it was clumsy to use; and it allowed too much anonymity. All of these factors deterred serious users, and many members fled to Facebook.

MySpace isn't dead. It has attempted to remake itself with a tighter focus on music and entertainment, carving a niche for itself in social media among musicians and bands. However it survives in that new garb (and it has serious competition from others like bandcamp), it lost its original momentum, and is no longer at the forefront of social networking.

Google+, on the other hand, is in the running. It started in mid-2011 with the advantage of having integration with Gmail, Picasa, search, and other Google services that already had a respectable user base. It built on and enhanced several of Facebook's and Twitter's earlier successes, growing to about 40 million users within six months of public launch. Google also benefits from its integration with the Android operating system that powers many of today's smartphones and tablets.

Google+ puts a new, but not exotically different, spin on the community concept (called "circles") and has a video-chat feature called "hangout" that even offers screen-sharing capability. The "Sparks" feature is a mini-search engine that offers users a feed of internet news briefs based on your search keywords.

Google+ has a long way to go to rival Facebook's user base, but it doesn't have to achieve the numbers to be a success. Google's main property is metrics: it measures things. Google+ provides the company a new way to measure online social dynamics and monitor signals about what users believe is relevant or popular at any time, so it can incorporate that into its search engines. Bringing social media metrics into the search algorithms is vital for Google's future. Success, for Google, is in using Google+ to enhance and hone its search capabilities.

Even so, Google+ has already developed a healthy user base and a lot of loyal customers who like its look, feel, and services over its competitors. Many of its features set the bar higher for Facebook and other sites to match. Google recently dropped its "Buzz" sharing service to drive more of its Gmail users to Google+.

Flickr, Picasa, and SmugMug

Photo-sharing sites are like YouTube, but with a focus on static images rather than video (although most allow some video content). These services are somewhat less popular since Facebook and other social networks developed and improved their own intrinsic photo galleries. For many users, however, these photo-sharing sites are preferable to the larger social network sites because they do not claim ownership of the content posted on them.

The big difference between Flickr and Picasa (aka PicasaWeb) is the interface focus. Flickr is more aimed at community interaction and sharing, while Picasa is focused more on managing and arranging your photos. Flickr has a tag feature to allow users to identify people and places in photographs.

SmugMug is even more tightly focused on the photos, with limited community interaction.

Yahoo's Flickr is the most popular, followed by Google's Picasa. Both are free for basic use, but have limits on what you can upload. To get more space, and hide the advertising, you must purchase a premium account plan. SmugMug has no free service and offers video uploads in its high-end packages only.

Flickr has another advantage in that it has numerous third-party applications that work to connect Flickr with other programs and websites, making it much easier to use the service outside the Flickr site.

Competitors include Photobucket, Shutterfly, Slide, Zooomr, Webshots, and Snapfish. Many of today's content management systems and forum packages also have photo gallery add-ons, and there are numerous open-licence (free) gallery programs you can install on your own server.

Unless you already have an existing account with one of these services, or you have a lot of photos to manage and need the additional tools, you can probably use Facebook's gallery feature for most of your photograph displays. Facebook also offers the option of "tagging" – identifying people and places in a photograph and sharing those tags with others.

Other Interactive Sites

There are tens of thousands of sites where you can communicate, share, and engage in debate. These include news media sites where you can comment on stories and editorials; and forums and bulletin boards where you can join topic "threads." Most photo galleries today have some aspect of social interaction, such as sharing, rating, and commenting on images. Blogs allow users to rate posts and comment on them.

Some sites, like <Stik.com>, are a collation of applications that use other sites (in this case Facebook) to create smaller social networks with specific target audiences, such as the students in your class, or members of a municipal department. They can be used to create communities for hobby and recreational groups, service clubs, or event organizers. The advantage is that the communities are smaller, more manageable, and easier to contain compared to the larger sites.

Google Earth has a collaborative component that lets users tag places, write descriptions, and even post their photographs to share with other users. Google Places lets you add place names and business addresses to Google Maps, which then become searchable by anyone using Google Maps (e.g., <walkscore.com>).

While you can add numerous social bookmarking links to your site to show how well connected you are, it's easy to overdo it. One news site I visited in researching this book had a pop-out window with 335 sites listed! Use a shorter list, especially for local or municipal sites.

It is the ubiquitous interlinking and sharing of content that makes social networking so successful. Many of the above sites use apps to connect with a major player like Facebook or Google+, thus enhancing that linked site's feel as a home base for interaction. Some connect with Twitter and place a link to their site directly into your tweet so you can tell others about it. Some other social networking sites are explored below.

eBay

eBay has social networking through its buyer and seller rating system. This lets the community identify problem or exemplary users. Peer pressure to get a good rating tends to encourage users to behave in an acceptable manner. It has a peer-to-peer conflict resolution system and eBay only steps in to adjudicate when that fails. eBay has incorporated a consumer review system for new products, as well.

eBay also introduced the "trust economy" to the internet, where you send money to a stranger – an individual, not a store or business that can be held accountable through legislation – and get something in return. That this worked at all was so surprising that it was the subject of an article in *Scientific American* in 2007. It *does* work, thanks to the peer-rating system. Trust is part of the social network foundation, not just a tool for expanding business.

Amazon

Amazon was a pioneer in social media in many crucial areas. First, it allowed consumers to rate and review products, which sparked an often heated dialogue between reviewers and created a competition as to who was the most prolific or the most literate reviewer. Then, Amazon branched out from books to other products, which widened its consumer base, and at the same time included customer-created video reviews, as well as written. Today, Amazon is often visited by consumers who simply want to read the reviews when shopping for products. Amazon account holders can also create lists of their favourite items, such as "My 10 favourite books for a deserted island."

Nielsen's September 2011 survey showed 68 percent of social media users "go to social networking sites to read product reviews, and over half use these sites to provide product feedback …" It also showed 60 percent used these sites for product information, and 58 percent to get promotions or coupons. Amazon is the granddaddy of the user-review sites.

Amazon's other contribution is in electronic publishing: its worldwide market for electronic books (e-books) gave authors who could not find commercial publishers or afford self-publishing a new market for their works. Electronic publishing also provides authors with immediate feedback from purchasers in the way of comments and reviews, as well as offering a ranking system based on sales that authors can use to see if their works gain or lose popularity.

Amazon extended the reach of its social networking by adding its recommendation feature. Its "Customers who bought this item also bought ..." proved a popular way to sell more books because it felt like a peer or friendly recommendation, rather than a sales pitch.

Wikipedia and Other Wikis

The idea behind Wikipedia and all other wikis is information collaboration. These aren't social media *per se*, but rather collaborative encyclopedia sites where numerous contributors collectively build information pages for common use. This sort of peer review can help keep wikis objective and unbiased, but it can also lead to confusion, uncoordinated entries, and heated argument over "facts."

In a community, a wiki can provide a repository for oral history that would otherwise be lost when people move or pass away. These sites are not very difficult to create, but take some effort to maintain and complete. Services like wikispaces host free wikis, as well as offering premium, paid services.

Wikis can be very specific – about a particular game or place – or wide-ranging like Wikipedia, which has a stated goal of trying to bring together all of the knowledge of humankind. Wikipedia currently has almost 20 million articles on it (almost four million of them in English) and roughly 90,000 regular contributors.

Wikis can be stand-alone or incorporated within an existing website (usually within a content management system package – see Appendix A). Wikis work best if a group of dedicated volunteers contribute and moderate them regularly. Wikis can incorporate photos and video, as well as text.

Some sites are semi-wikis. The IMDB (Internet Movie Database) has information about films (cast, directors, lengths, etc.); but also allows users to add their own reviews, lists, and ratings for films. It also has a comment feature for users to post their opinions about reviews and other content.

Games, MMORPGs, and Virtual Worlds

It may seem way off-topic to list online games with social media, but it isn't really that farfetched. Many of the leading massive multiplayer on-line role-playing games (MMORPGs) have significant elements of so-cial networking built in. Many overt and subtle motivators are built into these games to encourage interaction and communication with others.

World of Warcraft, with over 11 million players, is the leader in the so-cial gaming experience.

Many of the games advertised on Facebook are socially interactive and require input from your Facebook friends to achieve specific goals or get rewards. These tend to foster cooperation and even collaboration in lei-sure activities.

Another kind of social gaming activity is the virtual social world. In these rich, virtual environments, users (called residents) interact through 3D characters called avatars. They can talk, buy and sell property, build homes and other objects, and interact. The largest virtual world, Second Life, allows complex interactions, including a limited kind of sexual contact among adult members.

Several real nations – the Maldives, Estonia, Sweden, Albania, and others – have opened virtual embassies in the Second Life world to dis-cuss visas, trade issues, and diplomacy with the residents.

Unlike games, virtual worlds have no specific objectives or goals. These worlds are "sandbox" simulations, similar to the solo computer game series, The Sims, except they feature multiplayer environments that en-courage user interaction.

One of the trends in social gaming is brand placement and integration within the games. Achieving certain game goals can earn you coupons for fast food restaurants, discounts at online stores, etc. Social gamers can also purchase virtual products within their game – to enhance the game experience itself – and estimates suggest social gamers will buy $6 billion in virtual goods by 2013.

Social Bookmarking

If social media is a galaxy, social bookmarkers are the constellations that bind them into patterns. These services allow users to share what they've found online, usually through links to the sites of interest. Like most social media, these lists can be shared publicly or limited to your networks. Members can also rate items, creating a peer ladder based on how other members vote for a story.

Items are categorized by topic and can also be searched. The standard display is by popularity, with the hottest items at the top of the page, but the positioning can change as members rank their favourites through votes.

You can bookmark sites through Facebook, Twitter, Google+, and others (by sharing a link in a post on your wall or profile page); but these sites are not specific to bookmarking. Bookmarking sites have software to rate and rank the results, displaying the items rated top to bottom, based on how members vote. They can organize bookmarks by topic, keyword, and geography.

Among the most popular social bookmark sites are Digg, Delicious, and Pinterest. These aggregate content tagged (or "dug" in the case of Digg; pinned in the case of Pinterest) by their members as worthy of being shared.

Summary

At any time, newcomers might grab the brass ring of widespread popularity. New technologies or platforms can come forward and capture the fickle public's attention. Look at what Facebook did to Friendster and MySpace in a very short time. But, as these major social sites grow in use, they also grow exponentially in costs to run.

The hardware required to maintain even a modestly popular social media site is more than what most individuals or small entrepreneurs can afford. It takes a corporation with significant financial resources and a serious business plan to offset costs and maximize revenue for a site like Facebook or Google+. That won't change any time soon.

Nor do people really want it to. An Insites Consulting survey found 66 percent of internet users don't want any new social networks; 93 percent are happy with what they have and don't intend to change sites. As Facebook and Google+ grow, the smaller social network sites will need to become more niche-oriented micro-networks in order to survive.

Forums that were once the focal point of online communities are at the greatest risk of becoming redundant, as members flock to Facebook.

Many online forums, for example, have seen their membership dwindle in the past two or three years.

To retain their audience, successful traditional media have adopted social networking components on their websites. Some of these include bookmarking stories; others link the story to your Twitter and Facebook accounts, so you can share it via a tweet or status update. Most allow users to comment on stories and editorial opinions.

There are new social networking sites and services being developed all the time, many aimed at a niche audience, or that work as subsets of other social media sites. How well they survive, what emerges from the creative minds of developers, and who ends up on top in five years is anyone's guess.

Chapter 6

What Results Can You Expect from Participation?

Social media has uses similar to those of traditional media, but with a wider audience and often a very different way of achieving results. Social media is interactive and collaborative, so anything can spark a response.

The biggest difference between traditional media and social media is that, with social media, you deal directly with the end user – with the people who read, comment on, and follow your posts, and who are most affected by what you say and do. You don't go through the intermediary of another service like a newspaper or TV network. And, the reverse is true as well: the end user gets to post back to the content provider directly, without intermediaries.

Expectations from media interactions were discussed in my previous book, *Politically Speaking: Media Relations & Communication Strategies for Municipal Politicians* (Municipal World, 2012), but this chapter deals specifically with the results you can expect from social media.

Decide first if you expect the audience to respond and, if so, when. Now? Later? Never? What do you do if you get that response? What if you don't get it? What size or type of response constitutes success? How do you measure influence and engagement? Are the numbers of comments, subscribers, or followers your indicators? If so, how do you calculate them? And who does all this work?

Once you have determined the response, you can prepare to achieve that goal.

You can expect three basic results from any traditional media activity: information, action, and engagement. These apply equally to your on-line activity; but, a fourth result is unique to social media: influence. Of course, you can expect (or achieve) a combination of these as well, not merely one of them.

FYI: For Information Purposes Only

Information means informing the public of an event, issue, decision, or upcoming matter. While the message is static and passive, your main expectation is that it gets shared.

Information is important – politicians need to keep their constituents informed about a myriad of topics. Sometimes, it's self-aggrandizing: telling the public what you did on their behalf. That is not entirely self-serving because, as a public representative, you have a responsibility to keep the public informed about how their tax dollars are being used and about decisions that affect them.

Municipalities also have events and issues to present: changes to by-laws, garbage pickup, parking fees, planning meetings, upcoming public events, and other activities. Sharing information in a passive manner is not the greatest strength of social media. You may be better off using static websites, blogs, traditional media, or other forms of distribution if you want to inform the public in depth about administrative issues. However, because of its large audience, social media can be a good place for keeping local users informed in brief content.

This can be very effective if you have a large body of non-permanent residents in your municipality ("weekenders," cottagers, and part-timers). Publishing notices of planning meetings or asking for input on proposed by-law changes in the local media is fine for your permanent residents; but, if you also post a notice on your Facebook page, you can reach outside your community to those non-permanent residents who may be equally affected. The same applies with putting the notice into a tweet.

However, even what you see as a bland announcement, not intended to generate any response, might stir up comment and reaction in social media.

Do online comments constitute a valid comment under your provincial laws? Probably not, although that could change. People may expect that making a comment about a planning issue on your Facebook page has the same credibility as making the same comment to council or staff by mail or email. It may require some intervention to get the commenter to put those words into a format acceptable to your provincial requirements in order to have them included in any public record.

Getting the Audience to Act or Respond

Action means you expect someone or some organization to respond. Calling for the province or municipality to preserve a local, threatened wetland is a call for action (as well as a call for community engagement – see below).

Dissenters and protestors have successfully used Facebook, blogs, Twitter, and YouTube to get their message across and demand action on many issues. While calls for action can be seen as confrontational, they may also represent the forefront of a popular movement or sentiment. Confrontation can galvanize support, but also runs the risk of polarizing the community.

Grassroots movements can be created by mixing action and engagement to get others equally passionate about the issue. Social media energizes the groundswell into widespread action. The organizers of the recent "Occupy Wall Street" movement successfully galvanized thousands of protestors worldwide to stage similar events in their community by using social media. Many of the popular uprisings in the Middle East were spurred through social media.

Action can be a call for attendance at a public meeting or a community event. Something as prosaic as a planning meeting can be announced through your social network, as well as in traditional media.

An expected action might be as simple as getting viewers to click on links to another site where more information is provided. The number of "click-throughs" is fairly easy to measure.

Engaging the Community

Engagement lies between action and information. You want others to get involved on behalf of your issues and interests: the public, other councillors, other municipalities, other organizations. That doesn't necessarily mean you're demanding an immediate resolution to an issue or a specific action. Users of social media who become engaged will help share your cause and spread it around. They take some ownership of the issue.

This is also called "crowd-sourcing" – harnessing the enthusiasm and talents of outsiders to contribute towards your goal. It also means, according to Wikipedia, "sourcing tasks traditionally performed by specific individuals to an undefined large group of people or community (crowd) through an open call."

"Social media's promotion of community values can motivate people to take action that can help everyone in that community to succeed," writes John Blossom in *Content Nation*. He adds, "Highly profitable, long-lasting relationships can be built through social media that can enable communities to succeed together."

Communities, in this case, don't necessarily equate with municipalities, but can be groups within a municipality or a region as well.

Sometimes, a call for engagement is a way to measure public opinion. If no one responds, perhaps no one cares. One the other hand, sometimes it goes viral – like the "Occupy Wall Street" movement, taking on a life of its own outside the virtual reality of the internet. Online petitions have also become popular as engagement tools, using social media to reach potential signatories.

Sometimes, engagement means others will take your issue to a conclusion you neither expected nor wanted. That's the nature of online democracy.

"Activists are using social media to engage in politics around the clock, opening up opportunities for people who want to be involved, but whose commitments to job and family don't always fit within the typical late evening and weekend campaign schedule," wrote Steve Pearson of the political action committee ProjectVirginia. "Delivering a candidate's message with the click of a mouse doesn't diminish the importance of also delivering that message door-to-door, but it does help a campaign to cover a lot more ground with greater detail and frequency. Campaigners who provide social media tools to their online activist base are engaging a whole new political asset."

You can be actively engaged and participate in the conversations, or passively engaged – monitoring, but not contributing to them. However, passive engagement does not contribute to your influence.

Generating Influence

"Social media is about the people! Not about your business," wrote Matt Goulart of <webstarcontent.com>. He's right, but there's more to it; it's really about the relationship those people have with one another and with the content. Social media gives people some say in the relevance and distribution of the content. This is a huge change from the past, where specialized companies controlled both the content and its reach.

Social media is about the connections and relationships between people. Online, people can share information, experiences, ideas, thoughts, photographs, news, and more. People use social media to be together and to act together in ways that time and geography do not otherwise allow. It creates a sense of both shared experience and shared space.

Social media influence is a nebulous concept, and how it's measured is a topic of great debate among marketers and analysts. What it mainly entails is how well and often you participate, and what connections you make in the process. See Chapter 14 for more on measuring influence.

You likely have one primary goal among these four results, but any message or media interaction can include a mix of them. Because anyone can respond, you must remain focused and control your social media message to keep it from being misunderstood, abused, or hijacked. There is often more work in monitoring and maintaining messages online than through traditional media or static websites. And, because so many others can participate in the discussion, it is almost inevitable that someone will attribute their own slant to issues and take the conversation in unexpected directions.

Chapter 7

Security and Safety Online

Almost since the advent of the PC, there have been computer viruses. The first recorded virus is the "Elk Clone" virus from 1982, written by a 15-year-old high school student to infect Apple II computers through pirated software. Since then, tens of thousands have emerged, their spread made easier and more efficient by the internet. Confidentiality and privacy are not the only things at risk online.

Pirated software today is almost guaranteed to have a virus embedded in it, sometimes more than one. Viruses change faster than the antivirus software developers can update their products. Cybercrime is rampant.

You cannot safely operate any computer online without an up-to-date antivirus program running constantly. Even then, you need to use both caution and common sense when surfing the internet.

Viruses are only one challenge to security, however; hostile websites load spyware, malware, and adware that hijack your home page and steal passwords and other private information. Keyloggers can record your keystrokes and transmit them to outside computers to tell the hackers what you typed – a good way to uncover credit card numbers or access codes to online accounts or banking.

Email scammers send realistic-looking messages that appear to be from your bank, Paypal, your internet provider, or a credit card company, asking you to log on to a website and provide your username and password for "verification." Some of these scam emails and their sites look identical to the legitimate items. This is called "phishing."

If you have a social media account, you may receive email from people purporting to be on your friends list, or from Twitter accounts you follow. Usually, these phishing attempts provide links to sites that load harmful programs onto your system.

Malware – hostile computer programs – turn off your security settings, corrupt files, even wipe out hard drives. Some read your address list and send email under your name to your contacts, suggesting recipients open infected files or visit unsafe websites. A story in *Wired* magazine estimated that antivirus researchers uncover 12 million pieces of malware every year.

Hackers steal confidential files and private data by breaking into websites. They have stolen confidential – even top-secret – data from government and military sites. It's serious enough that the U.S. set up Cyber Command, a military agency subordinate to the U.S. Strategic Command. Its mission is to "direct the operations and defense of specified Department of Defense information networks, and prepare to, and when directed, conduct full spectrum military cyberspace operations in order to enable actions in all domains, ensure U.S./Allied freedom of action in cyberspace, and deny the same to our adversaries."

Many security analysts say Chinese hackers have compromised the security of every major North American corporation. While the Chinese government has denied this charge, and denies all involvement in the attacks, China is pinpointed by security agencies and by many Western governments as a force in the cyberwar that rages silently online.

And, this doesn't even list the tens of thousands of criminal attacks and identity-theft attacks that happen weekly. It's pretty scary. But, you can take precautions to help protect yourself. Here are a few:

➤ Keep your antivirus software on at all times when you use your computer. While antivirus programs are not 100 percent effective, they provide basic security. Keep them updated with the latest security patches.

➤ Where possible, use a router with a firewall to protect your online systems. At the very least, use a software firewall. (This is part of today's operating systems, usually active by default, or managed by your antivirus program; but, it never hurts to check to make sure it was not turned off by mistake or by malware.)

➤ Don't open any email attachments unless they are from someone you trust. You can ask for confirmation it was sent to you before you take any action. Before opening anything, save it to a disk and scan it with your antivirus program.

➤ Don't click on links in any email unless you know the sender or recognize the site. Put your mouse cursor over the link and see if the URL address that shows in the status bar matches the address of the link. If it doesn't, it may connect to a hostile site.

➤ Don't answer emails or posts that offer prizes, contests, or free, entertaining quizzes. Most of these lead to malware sites.

➤ Don't click on the "tiny" or "ow.ly" URL in a tweet or post of anyone you don't know or trust, especially in an email. These abbreviated links can lead to malware sites used in phishing scams. URL shorteners make tweeting much easier, but be aware of their potential risk.

➤ Use multiple passwords for online accounts. Do not store these on your computer.

➤ Don't download any software except from recognized and reputable sites. Never, ever trust pirated torrent or warez software.

➤ Do not provide any credit card or confidential information to an online vendor except through a secure server (with URL addresses that begin with https instead of the usual http).

➤ Keep your operating system and programs up-to-date and patched. Security vulnerabilities get fixed through patches and updates. Use the automatic update option to make it easier.

➤ Scan your computer regularly for viruses. I recommend doing a complete scan weekly.

➤ If your computer seems to be slowing down, scan it thoroughly. Malware and viruses can affect a computer's performance and a sluggish system is often the first sign of infection.

➤ Do not answer online or email requests for cash, no matter how sympathetic you may feel to the sob story. Your "friend" wasn't really robbed while on vacation, and isn't waiting for his passport in some overseas hotel. Most likely, your friend's computer was hacked and you're receiving a scam notice sent by malware from the infected machine.

➤ Don't respond to emails requesting your login information – password, username, and so on. Social media and online gaming companies won't ask you for this via email.

➤ Back up any important data on your computer, including your operating system files, on a regular basis. Keep the backup in a safe place away from your computer. Modern operating systems have easy-to-use backup programs to simplify this process. Ask your IT people if you're not sure how to use it.

➤ Messages about your drunken photo on Facebook or images of you cheating are more scams. They take you to a fake site where you enter your username and password to see these impossible photographs and instead have your personal login information stolen.

➤ Do not put anything of a truly confidential nature in any social media profile.

Pay attention to media alerts and news pieces about online security issues. Sometimes, authorities know of a pending cyber-attack or emerging virus and can warn users about it. Ask your IT department to share any news or warnings with all of your council and staff.

Chapter 8

Confidentiality and Privacy Issues

There's a famous cartoon from the *New Yorker* that shows a dog at a computer, saying to its canine companion, "On the internet, no one knows you're a dog." The joke has a lot of truth in it: the internet allows both anonymity and artificiality. You can be invisible. You can create an alternate personality. For a while, at least.

In mid-2011, Amina Arraf, a blogger alleging to be a Syrian feminist and lesbian, who commented about the problems of being female and homosexual in an Islamic nation, vanished. She had become a popular icon in the Syrian uprising, a rallying point for freedom of expression and for local activists. In June, a post on her blog claimed Arraf had been kidnapped by Syrian authorities in Damascus.

Activists, bloggers, and even officials anxiously searched for Amina, fearing she had become a victim of the regime. After investigation, some unsettling facts were exposed. The "Gay Girl in Damascus" as the blog was titled, turned out to be Thomas MacMaster, a 40-year-old straight, married American man and student at Edinburgh University. Investigators quickly turned up detailed information about his home, his wife, and his work.

MacMaster later apologized for his deception and deleted his blog; but, other writers claimed he "left a damper on the work of activists on the ground, social media and the role it is playing in this year of Arab revolutions, and the credibility of the Arab blogosphere …" and that he had "put the Syrian gay community at risk."

On the internet, no one knows you're a middle-aged, white suburbanite pretending to be a gay Syrian woman, either.

But, deception is hard to maintain. Someone will find out not only who you are, but also where you live and where you work. It is not difficult to trace you. Each computer connected to the internet identifies itself by a unique IP (Internet Protocol) address. Website registration is easy to uncover. Savvy people know how to find you. But, if you don't do anything illegal, stupid, immoral, or deceptive, there's little incentive for them to hunt you.

Posting Personal Information

Most social media encourage you to create a profile with a considerable amount of personal information about your past, your education, family, interests, favourite books and movies, and location. That helps the sites customize which ads you see and point you in the direction of games, events, friends, other pages, and so on. And, of course, it helps identify you.

Peter Cashmore, CEO of Mashable, wrote, "Privacy is dead, and social media hold the smoking gun." Writing in a guest opinion piece for CNN in 2009, he added, "We're living at a time when attention is the new currency: With hundreds of TV channels, billions of websites, podcasts, radio shows, music downloads, and social networking, our attention is more fragmented than ever before.

"Those who insert themselves into as many channels as possible look set to capture the most value. They'll be the richest, the most successful, the most connected, capable, and influential among us. We're all publishers now, and the more we publish, the more valuable connections we'll make."

That doesn't mean you have no privacy; just that privacy is not absolute. The social perception of privacy is changing. In essence, social networking makes the whole world into your neighbourhood – and your neighbours are peering into your windows. So, what about you is really confidential? Your credit card number and banking access codes? Of course you want to keep these private. But, is the name of the high school you attended really confidential? The city where you live? Your favourite movie? Your cat's name?

Several hundred million people online have already decided this is not critical information to be kept private. Social media has changed how personal information is perceived and managed.

Protecting Your Privacy

Every social media site does some sort of data mining. How much, what is done with it, how much gets stored, where it ends up, and even whether it gets sold or transferred to outside agencies depends on the site or service. Privacy issues have plagued social media sites ever since their inception. You cannot avoid having some of your information shared; but, you can actively restrict personal data by not entering it or being sure to engage any privacy option the site offers.

Mining your preferences or profile isn't new. Long before the internet, credit card companies were using your buying record to create a statistical image of your habits, to help target their marketing. Social media is an evolution of that, although it's not necessarily a commercial organization looking at your profile.

Even allegedly private conversations between members may not really be private. These are usually accessible by administrators or sysops. The service where these conversations took place will store and retain them. You have no control over how long they are kept or how they are used.

The safest thing to do is not to trust in the site's security or promises of confidentiality, but rather to make sure you post nothing in your profile, or anywhere on the site, that you do not wish to be made public.

Social media sites give you several levels of privacy and allow you to determine who can see your personal details, posts, photos, tweets, and so on. This can be open, fully allowing everyone to view all content, or restricted in various degrees to "friends," networks, circles, groups, or other approved audiences.

Hackers may attempt to get at your personal data and make it public. This "doxing" can be done by accessing your email, cellphone, social network, domains registered to you, and other sources. Loss of personal or confidential information is certainly a risk for everyone online.

The sheer volume of material online means that most of what you post may simply be ignored by other users, even if your content is fully accessible. But, the software behind the scenes is reading it, parsing it, and creating an index about you, your tastes, and your status. You can see this is good or bad, an invasion of your privacy, or a whole new world of openness. Success on social media comes through connections, and connections come from shared information, much of it personal. That's why the default button for sharing is "everyone" – you can select a restricted range from a menu if you want a post to be private.

As an exercise, before you sign up for a social media account, do a search on your own name – use quotation marks around your name like this: "John Smith" and add your town or city. See what comes up. You may be surprised by how much is already online and easily accessible through a search engine. Check <knowem.com> and <checkusernames.com> for usernames you have accounts under, and <com.lullar.com> for your email address to see where it was registered.

Prepare to Share

When you use social media, be prepared to share. You will not get anything out of it unless you are willing to put something in, but decide how much information to give out when you create a profile on a social media site. It's up to you to be diligent about what you post and who you allow to see it, not the site where you fill in the forms. Treat social media like an open book and only post what is appropriate.

Many social networking sites, including forums, blogs, and news media sites, allow you to create an anonymous or at least artificial persona. You can choose a different user name that others see; use a fake photograph and an anonymous email account. But why bother? As an elected official, your strength lies in being recognized and being part of the dialogue, not hidden from it or sniping from the shadows.

You might be able to create a fake persona and get away with the deception for a while, but when it intersects with other peoples' lives, someone will find out who you really are.

In general, real anonymity is counterproductive in social media. It restricts your ability to connect with friends, family, co-workers, and others online unless they recognize your username. Anonymity and fake names may be prudent or necessary when protecting one's identity on whistleblower sites, sites that encourage reviews of or comments on local businesses or your workplace, or sites you have reason to believe are monitored by unfriendly government agencies. They are also common on sites that allow comments on news stories where political views get aired.

Google+ requires you to use your real name, not an artificial one. While there are ways of getting around that requirement, the intent is to raise the level of the conversations by letting people know with whom they are talking. Similarly, LinkedIn and Facebook encourage real names.

You have the choice not to post anything you don't want made public or repeated in other media or other sites. If you really want a private conversation, use the phone.

Since Facebook was used to post pictures of looters and those engaged in vandalism after riots in Vancouver and England, there has been a vigorous debate going on about online privacy and appropriate use of social media. The public was asked to help law enforcement agencies to identify the accused and, as a result, hundreds of charges were laid. Were the rights of the accused violated by being shown without the benefit of legal process? Should social media serve the state?

The debate continues, but won't be solved any time soon. Lawmakers at higher levels of government will have to wrestle with the impact of social media on our societies. Pay attention to what comes from both federal and provincial authorities, and participate in the discussions if you have the opportunity.

Chapter 9

Other Social Media Risks

The hype plays up the benefits of social media, but there are clearly risks in using it, too. Privacy and confidentiality were discussed in the last chapter, but there are other issues to consider.

The anonymity that allows people more freedom to speak their minds and express concerns without fear of reprisal also allows political opponents and rivals to masquerade under assumed identities to challenge and ridicule other politicians. This is more prevalent at the federal and provincial levels, where party politics are adversarial. But, it does happen at the municipal level and such attacks can prove damaging to your campaign. It can be even more damaging to the credibility of the person whose campaign team is caught engaging in such underhanded methods, however.

Some social media sites place more emphasis on using real names and identifying users. Others have been criticized because they have allowed sufficient anonymity that sexual predators have been active on them. That's unlikely on sites like Facebook and Google+, but not impossible.

Managing Corporate Pages

Page management is a risk. Facebook only allows one profile to be associated with a page. If your municipality has multiple pages, one person within your organization will have to take responsibility for creating a profile that manages all the organization's pages. It's either that or have multiple staff people managing different pages.

Profiles are designed to carry personal information and to link with other people. That individual will have personal and intimate ties to the pages, and thus to the organization. This puts that person in a position of authority, with a fair amount of responsibility. A high level of trust is required by the organization, too.

Other social networking sites are similar: aimed at individual use, not organizations. Even when you have a group or corporate account (Twitter, for example), it's usually assigned to one person.

If your staff maintain municipal pages using their own profiles, when does the job end? Where is the boundary between their personal life and their work? If they post on Facebook after work hours, are they posting as themselves or as employees? If they answer a question or post on the corporate site after hours, are they working – and thus deserve some compensation for that work – or posting as an individual?

Life and work mesh on social media in ways that are difficult to untangle. HR departments may have to update job descriptions to include a section about online work after hours and be clear if there will be compensation for same.

The person with the Facebook profile has all of the "friends" – they stay with profiles, and can't be ported over to Facebook pages. There are ways to transfer the ownership of pages to others on Facebook (making other users as administrators is one method), but there is no simple way to transfer friends. But, whose friends are they – the organization's or the individual's? Probably, it's a bit of both. In order to clarify the relationship, the profile holder needs to use the Facebook list feature that lets him or her create specific categories for friends.

Posting on a Facebook page you own means you can post under that page's name (which can be a municipality, department, event, etc.), as well as using a different profile picture for that page. This helps reduce some of the confusion between individual and corporation. An individual politician can also create a page that is separate from the profile name. It might be called something like "John Smith, Regina Council," with a different image used for posts made there.

Defining Limits and Responsibilities

Spell out the limits and the responsibilities of such links and networks in your social media policy. Who controls the user name and password?

What happens if the person is ill, is on vacation, or leaves the job? Is the profile linked to a corporate or private email address? Who can close or take over the account if it's abandoned? What will you do if the owner abuses the account and posts inappropriate material? Who else monitors the account holders?

In late 2011, a news story told about a former employee being sued by his ex-employers for taking his Twitter followers with him after he left the company; the company claimed the followers belonged with the job, not the person. To avoid that situation in your municipality, have your IT department ensure that all corporate Twitter, Facebook, and other social network accounts are linked to your municipal email addresses, and not to personal accounts.

Posting inappropriate material is a risk since it threatens to damage the municipality's reputation or brand. Sharing proprietary or copyright content on a social media site will be problematic. (See Appendix D and read the particular site's terms of use as well.)

With all this connectivity, we have come to expect a 24/7 information flow. People get very upset when they don't receive an email response to a complaint or a query within a day. Adding social media monitoring and responding can put a lot of stress on both you and municipal staff. Will you need someone new to deal with social media, rather than burdening existing staff?

Who is the best person to deal with social media? The tech-savvy 20-something with little or no work experience, or the veteran staffer who may not be as fast or as up-to-date with technology, but has years of experience dealing with customer service and relations with residents? Managing social media may require less technical expertise than you think. Assigning the task to someone experienced in dealing with the public might be a better choice.

Having to monitor and maintain a lot of sites leads to social media fatigue (aka "stream fatigue"). People get tired, bored, and fed up if work becomes monotonous. Better to focus on a limited number of potentially useful sites than spread yourself too thin over every possible networking site. When readers get fatigued, they start "unliking," "unfollowing," and "unfriending" you to reduce their stream of input.

Fatigue sets in, too, when you have many accounts to oversee or too many sites to track. Keeping up with conversations on Facebook alone can be time-consuming, but throw in Twitter, LinkedIn, YouTube, and several blogs – and you have a full day's work just reading.

The empowerment of every person to be a content provider is an exciting development in the history of democratic engagement. But, trying to heed so many voices, so many opinions, in so many directions, and over so many channels can be disastrous. You can get overwhelmed by the sheer volume of content. You work so hard to stay up-to-date and in touch that you cease to be an effective leader. You end up working for the social media, when it really should work for you.

Errors, Omissions, Defamation, and Libel

Poor grammar skills are another risk. Not only is clear, correct, and concise writing necessary for effective communication, but others will judge you when you make mistakes. There is no reason any municipality should post anything that is not grammatically correct and properly spelled.

What happens if you or a staff person posts something incorrect or misleading? Even if it was done unintentionally (for example, typing May 24 as a date for a public meeting when the actual date was May 14), there may be legal implications. That's one reason it helps to have someone with reasonable keyboarding and English skills to do the posting.

Defamation and libel are serious considerations when posting online. While it might seem like common sense not to post anything that could be considered libelous, people get carried away and sometimes forget they are not alone when online. I wrote earlier that you can challenge an issue that comes up at the table, but should avoid challenging individuals or their decisions. Even if what you say is not libelous, it might be considered defamatory by someone eager to launch a legal fight.

In October 2011, the Supreme Court of Canada ruled that linking to a website containing links to libelous material does not in itself constitute libel. The court recognized a difference between simply linking to a website and "actively encouraging someone to follow a link to a website with defamatory content." However, posting defamatory content from the hyperlinked material would constitute publishing by the hyperlinker, and thus be open to legal action.

Tweeting or posting on Facebook during a meeting may be annoying, even if not illegal; but, if it happens during an closed meeting, it can overstep the bounds of your confidentiality agreement and even shift into illegality. It's another section that needs to be included in your social media policy.

Some people find social networking addictive, and may pursue it at the expense of job and family life. Once online, they find it difficult to get away. They "like" many pages and accept almost every friend request to get the feed. They comment on or "like" most of the posts. They join groups and play social games like Farmville. They skip meals and breaks to stay online. They avoid other work in order to be connected through social sites. Internet addiction is a documented illness, and well beyond the scope of this book to discuss. Managers and administration should be aware that some staff can fall prey to it, and usage should be monitored. Help staff keep their work and private personas separate.

Measuring Success and Being Accountable

If you or your municipality invests time, resources, and money into developing your social media presence, how do you determine your success or failure? Counting "likes" and "friends" does not necessarily add up to a meaningful metric. Influence and engagement are notoriously slippery to quantify. Participating in social media involves a risk that there will be no concrete, measurable result, and no return on investment that you can put into a spreadsheet.

It will certainly reduce your perceived risk if you have a business plan with clearly defined goals before you invest into social media. Simple goals – for example, to improve communications and provide residents with a method to interact and comment – will make it easier to measure your success, and you won't have to balance any return on investment in quantifiable figures. If you want to measure something like reach, influence, and engagement, you really have to measure both your own status and that of everyone networked to you. It's a complicated challenge that, so far, no one has overcome satisfactorily. Companies are working to create quantifiable solutions, but no one has come up with generic measurements that work for every user.

Bandwidth hogging can be another risk. If a lot of staff are browsing Facebook, Twitter, and other social media sites at the same time, they can reduce the bandwidth available for other users. This can cause a lowering of productivity for those staff who need online access.

Finally, for politicians, sacred cows and cherished agendas may be at risk. The public will call us to account for our campaign promises. The online public can be intolerant of partisan politics and bold about commenting on your performance. It can be humbling, even humiliating. But, you hope that, in dealing with everyone openly and evenly, you will gain some of their respect in return. The worst risk is that you can be ignored. Silence is not golden online; it's deafening.

Chapter 10

What Municipal Politicians Can Do

If the internet and social media are so fraught with danger and challenges, should politicians stay clear of them completely?

No. A chainsaw can be dangerous, too, if you don't use it correctly. If you're careful and plan well, social media is a toolbox of great potential that you can use to your advantage. Besides, you don't really have a lot of choice: using social media is necessary today.

Powerful Tool for Politicians

The marriage of politics and social media seems the perfect pairing: politicians with tools that enhance and expand their ability to connect and converse with the public. Social media provides politicians with an inexpensive but powerful platform from which to engage the public, to explain one's self, to promote visions, to encourage participation, and to advocate for issues.

As a politician, you have more freedom of expression than municipal staff have. That comes with an equal responsibility because you represent the municipality to the public. Even if many of the rules and constraints in the town's social media policy are not directed towards you, you should abide by their principles.

Blogger Josh Sternberg wrote on Mashable, "It used to be that most of us couldn't point out our local representative, councilman, alderman, or public advocate if we tripped over him or her, but that's starting to change, thanks to social media helping us raise our civic literacy levels and altering the way politics are [sic] done. We now expect our local representative for our state or town assembly or senate or council to connect with us on a more personal level. And, it's happening."

While he's writing about U.S. politics, Sternberg's sentiments are equally true in Canada. As a municipal politician, you are already close with your local citizens; you already have personal involvement with your community and its organizations. You already network in your town; social media helps extend and strengthen that network.

Social media can be a powerful political tool. Look at how it formed the backbone of the "Arab Spring" movement and continues to shape politics and events in the Middle East. It puts political debate on a personal level. Savvy politicians realize you have to be part of the discussion online or be shut out entirely. Even the nature of our offline conversations is increasingly being affected by our online conversations. Social media is even changing how we talk about communicating offline.

Michael Parent, business professor at Simon Fraser University, commented on the low use of social media by candidates in the 2010 Vancouver municipal elections: "What surprises me more (than candidates' lack of use) is that they haven't realized the power of being able to tap into communities through social media."

Parent added that social media provides a "good litmus test for their opinions or their positions, because the community will react quickly – either positively or negatively – to any message that goes out."

As John Blossom wrote in *Content Nation*, "Social media challenges politicians to use the empowerment of citizens to drive their own political power, a task that requires a willingness both to support and to engage in real conversations on real issues."

Developing Your Online Presence

Some of the following discussion is technical, so if you're not comfortable with that aspect, find someone to help guide you through these steps. And, unless you have those skills, you will also need to find someone to build and maintain your website.

The first thing to do is to create a Facebook profile and start letting people know about it. Ditto with profiles and accounts on Twitter, Google+, and LinkedIn (set these up at the very least; and add YouTube if you plan to post videos). List your website address and Twitter name on your business cards. And, if you really want to be in the forefront, include a QR code (see Appendix C).

As for usernames, keep them simple and memorable. Real names are preferable, but you may find a lot of people already registered with your name, and you really don't want to be called "johnsmith12345" or "Jane. Doe.123345." Nicknames like "saltydog14651" can be amusing when you create them; but, like tattoos, you must live with them long after your enthusiasm has waned. Find a username that reflects your role, like "Jane Smith Councillor." Use your initials, or (if allowed) characters like periods, space, underscore, or hyphens: "J.W.Smith_Councillor." Give your username some thought before you create an account – you may not be able to change it later.

A Facebook page is not the same as a Facebook profile. Individuals may need a profile only, but you can also create pages after you have a profile. Be careful with the settings in your profile. Social media includes numerous options for who sees what content – how various posts, comments and other content are shared. Sometimes, these are turned on by default, but offer you the ability to opt out of them and avoid having that content automatically made public.

Organizations will need one or more pages; but, individuals can create multiple pages, too. I have a page for my council political comments, and two more for other interests. However, because Facebook allows only one profile to be associated with a page, even if you have multiple pages, someone within your organization will have to take responsibility for creating a profile that manages the organization's pages.

Engaging Friends and Followers

With Facebook, Google+, and LinkedIn, you will want to invite others to join your group of contacts, and you will want to join theirs. Search for relevant or interesting groups to join, so you can join in those discussions, too. Use Facebook's "like" feature to associate yourself with relevant groups or communities. Every group you join, every page you become a fan of or like, every person you follow or befriend extends your network and your reach; it does the same for those whom you have befriended and followed. It's a mutually beneficial relationship.

With Twitter, you will need to start following others. Search for people, groups, municipalities, and organizations and follow them. To avoid being overwhelmed, use Twitter's list feature to organize your contacts (followers and following) into relevant categories. Advertise your identity and include it on your business cards. Soon, others will be following you.

If you link your Twitter account to your Facebook account, any tweet you make will also be replicated on Facebook. This cross-pollination of posts also helps improve your influence count on various social media metrics sites.

Facebook has a "subscribe" feature, similar to Twitter's "follow." Use it to keep track of people and organizations of interest to you (other politicians, municipalities, newscasters, etc.).

Use the social media site's calendar to keep readers informed of events and activities in which you are involved.

If you plan to blog, the easiest way is to open an account with a free blog service like Wordpress, Blogger, or Tumblr. These are relatively simple to set up, but will require technical assistance to customize and expand more fully. Alternatively, if you already have a website and a server, you could install blogging software on your server. This is more complicated and requires some technical knowledge to set up the database.

For your website, secure a domain for yourself – usually your own name, if it's available. It's a lot easier for people to find and recognize <bobsmith.com> or <janedoe.ca> than if you're buried within a collective service. Even if you don't use it right away, the cost to register and park a domain is minimal. If you want to build a website, many servers charge low annual fees to keep your domain online.

This domain can host a static page about yourself and your vision, or one that gets updated regularly with your activities, votes, motions, and accomplishments. You can include photographs or videos of you at local events. Your contact information should be easy to find. Your website can be as simple as a single page, or more complex, with multiple pages.

A more ambitious site will have interactive elements, including links to your Facebook, Twitter, and other social media profiles, "like" buttons and other related applets. You can also add a forum package on your own site. A forum just about you won't be very popular, so broaden its focus to encourage people to read and post on it. This also requires some technical expertise to set up, and a Facebook page may prove to be more active.

A separate domain can be left unused (parked) until an election, when you can use it as your campaign site. You can have a hidden back-end for communication and messaging that is used by your campaign team to organize, share comments, and plan your collective timetable. Social media is not just for elections, however, so don't drop it once you get into office!

Keeping the Momentum Going

Once you have your accounts established, you'll have to visit the sites regularly to post on them, check messages, read posts from others ("friends" and circles), and respond. Blogs require the most work because you need to keep them up-to-date and interesting. If you don't plan to visit your pages regularly (or simply can't), your online presence will stagnate.

In large political organizations, individual politicians seldom do this work. Staff set up and maintain the sites. Be careful, however, not to allow anyone other than you to post under your name.

Having these pages and sites is only the start. Web pages need to be optimized for search engines to find them. Social media sites depend on networks of friends and followers, so you need to initiate those contacts on each site. Sometimes, this is a simple point-and-click to request or accept a friend. You may have to create categories (Twitter's and Facebook's lists or the Google+ circles, for example) to organize your contacts or to specify which groups can see your posts. You can also restrict viewing of your photos and videos to specific groups using the list feature.

Let people know how to connect with you online. Let the traditional media know what your Twitter name is, where to find your Facebook page, and so on. If you send out newsletters to constituents, include your social media links. Be proactive by contacting local bloggers and putting them on your contact list for any news, updates, and Twitter feeds. Do the same with local media and fellow council members.

You need to become an influencer (see Chapter 14) – someone others turn to for ideas, information, recommendations, and conversations. To achieve this, you will have to participate in social networks actively, and develop a strong set of active connections. You will need to add value to the conversations, not just post a few bland words. Social media is a participatory culture where information is currency and networks are the infrastructure.

The greater your influence, the more your peers will pay attention to you, and the more interest your comments will generate among the media and online in the e-media.

Personal branding, or self-positioning, is a new concept Wikipedia defines as "... the process whereby people and their careers are marked as brands ... success comes from self-packaging." Politicians must market themselves to their communities all the time, particularly during election campaigns. Creating your online presence, staking your space in social media, and developing a role as an influencer all help solidify your personal brand.

Mitch Joel, in his book *Six Pixels of Separation,* writes, "The needs for autonomy, recognition, and achievement are essential to our sense of self-worth and are fulfilled in online communities, blogs, and social networks that provide a way to develop and manage a virtual reputation," wrote.

If you're already social media-savvy, bring your fellow members of council into the picture. Help them get set up on the popular sites; share your links and pages with them. This will strengthen your own network as much as it strengthens your group connections. You can even create a Facebook page for your council as a whole.

Create a Facebook group for regional politicians, a "by-invitation," restricted-access area where you can promote and discuss regional ideas. Or, think bigger: create a Facebook group for all municipal politicians in your province, where you can all share your ideas and thoughts.

Social media can be used for a wide range of networking opportunities that have so far seen little use. You could be the spark that lights it on fire for municipal politicians.

Chapter 11

Blogging for the Common Good

Web logs – now known as blogs – built the platform for citizen journalists to comment on and critique everything in their world. Blogs provide a simple, inexpensive method of publishing for everyone. Many opinions once reserved for coffee shop chatter or over-the-fence griping with the neighbour are now available online for everyone to read.

Blogging developed from simple online diaries into something much more powerful. Many blogs continue to be digital versions of personal journals and diaries. Others, however, focus on specific topics, such as politics, religion, technology, or science.

The importance of blogs to the public dialogue cannot be overstated. Opinion is no longer constrained to the editorial pages of the newspaper or to the scheduled commentaries of radio and TV journalists. The exclusivity of traditional media in sharing opinion has evaporated. Anyone can have their say and make it known to the rest of the world.

Whether that opinion attracts readers depends on the skill and talent of the writing. Blogs have allowed many people to publish what would never have been printed in newspapers; they made us all citizen publishers. Bloggers have particular impact in smaller communities where politics are more intimate.

Bloggers are seldom restricted by the rules that govern traditional media. Many blogs are simply virtual soapboxes for owners to rant and rave about the wrongs of the world. Caustic comments about people, issues, and ideas; personal attacks; and even libel that would not get play in traditional media – all these find a home in some blogs.

Politicians also blog, although not nearly in the numbers that their critics do. That, in my mind, is unfortunate. Politicians have traditionally had their activities and opinions presented to the public through the lens of the media. How good or how poor you appear in the media often depends on how much or how well the journalist understood the issue or your position, or your personal relationship with the reporter. Today, we may be seen through a blogger's eyes, as well as a reporter's.

Managing Your Own Message

Every politician has had the experience of being misquoted, misunderstood, or even misrepresented in a news story. That may be the result of a misheard word, an error in transcribing, a lack of knowledge about the issue, or a simple mistake. But, for the politician, it can hurt a reputation, damage credibility, and even sink a career. Damage control after the fact is seldom effective in repairing one's reputation.

As a politician, you benefit from a lot of information to which the public and the media have no access. The public really has no way to appreciate all of the time, effort, research, conversations, reading, and emailing that go into your decisions or your motions. All the public sees or hears is the final result of what is often a lengthy and convoluted process.

Most municipal politicians run for office for admirable reasons: to contribute, to help find solutions, to make a change for the better, to improve, and to accomplish things for the community. But, when we win our seats, we often find our voices are unheard. The media focuses on the mayor, and our comments, no matter how well thought out, are ignored. Issues we think to be pivotal get short shrift or go unreported. The public doesn't see or hear all the passion, enthusiasm, and commitment we have for our role.

How, then, do you keep the public informed? How do you explain your actions? How do you express yourself, engage the community, and let people know you are still passionate and committed to your role?

You can comment at the table, of course. If you have the budget, you can send out household flyers. Traditional media can publish your content. You can hold media conferences. You can send letters to the local newspapers or get interviewed on radio or TV.

When you want to move from publication to conversation, it's time to get into social networking.

You can, of course, create an account on Facebook, Twitter, or Google+ and post your thoughts there. These all restrict your posts to relatively small character counts – Twitter to a strict 140, while the others are more lenient – so you cannot provide any real depth (although you can link to outside articles). Links are the "currency of the web" and establish you not only within the network, but also count when search engines evaluate your pages' or posts' ranking.

Or, you can create a blog and put some depth into it. It's the one social media tool that allows you to put together content without restrictions on length, word count, or the size or number of images. Plus, it can be read by everyone, not just the selected friends or members of your pre-defined circles. While posts on Twitter and Facebook disappear from the screen pretty quickly, blog posts have great longevity and can be around for years.

Blogs add value and depth to any online conversation. Unlike many social media sites, they usually allow lengthy responses. Readers can engage in a much fuller discussion than the usual short bursts on Facebook or Twitter. People look for relevant, enriching content on blogs.

Blogs are also your own content, whereas the comments you place on a social network may not be (read their terms of service).

Choosing a Platform and Learning the Ropes

Creating a blog is easy today and most options are free. Several online platforms allow you to create a blog and start writing with very little technical know-how required (Blogger, Wordpress, and Tumblr, for example). For the more technically adept, downloadable packages can be run on a host server. These all allow you to create an individual blog.

The biggest challenge is getting your blog recognized, read, and responded to. With 175 million or so blogs already online, according to BlogPulse, you must say something meaningful to get a regular audience. Niche blogging (sticking to local issues, for example) is one way to stake your claim.

How do you learn to blog? Mostly by reading other people's blogs. With so many bloggers already online, you have no shortage of examples. Spend a week surfing the blogosphere and seeing how others do it. Look for how they use links, photos, and videos. Are their posts generally long or short? Do they quote others or link to news and other sites in their posts? Are posts serious dissertations or conversational pieces? Are layouts open and easy to read, or cluttered and dense? Do they have defined topics or use unique tags for each piece? Do they list their favourite blogs and other sites?

Figure out what you like and copy the best ideas.

Not every blog post is a literary masterpiece. Some are just short status updates, or a brief comment with links to interesting websites. If you're uncomfortable writing lengthy pieces, relax: your skills will improve with practice and it will become easier. Use the blog's draft feature to write your post; then, reread and edit it before publishing it. I read my longer posts aloud to my wife, then make corrections before I move them into public areas for others to see.

Linking to other news stories or commentaries also strengthens your place in the network. It shows connectivity, which is rated highly by search engine algorithms. That's why it never hurts to have a list of links to favourite sites (a "blogroll") on your home page.

Once you have your own blog up and running, search for aggregate sites that list (and sometimes reprint content from) blogs, and register your blog there. You will want to look for relevant associations: sites that list Canadian political or municipal blogs, for example. You may want to give these aggregate sites permission to reproduce your posts, to help spread your influence around. In most cases, the aggregators only reproduce basic content, and do not offer social networking features like comments or rating.

With a little creativity and some tinkering, you could actually create a group blog where everyone on your council could participate. Add-on blog packages work with many municipal websites (sites that run on content management systems), and allow everyone at the council table a space on the same server. Council blogs would all be available through the municipal website, for convenient public access.

This kind of system makes the posts very easy to find, convenient, and transparent. However, some council members and staff may see this as a can of worms they're afraid to open. Although blogs are often viewed as confrontational, they don't have to be so.

As a politician, you have a responsibility to keep your electorate informed. While blogging is an excellent tool for this purpose, it's hard work, even if it's ultimately enjoyable and fulfilling. You have to both write your material and maintain (and sometimes update) your site. According to Technorati, the average blogger spends 3.3 hours blogging every week. Can you afford that sort of commitment?

Blog-fade is what happens when a blogger starts off strong, then peters out, running out of things to say, time, or energy. It's also known as pod-fade, for podcasters who fail to keep up their efforts. It's likely your blogging output will wax and wane over time; but, don't let it die completely. If you can't think of anything significant to say, post something short, something easy, to keep readers aware you haven't fallen off the face of the earth.

Things to Consider

Consider the following caveats before you begin.

> You should be reasonably good at writing, or have someone who can proofread and edit it for you. Bad writing – poor grammar and bad spelling included – will hurt your credibility.

> Be consistent and post regularly. Nothing will kill your audience size faster than infrequent, sporadic, unfocused posts. Expect to post at least once a week to maintain any regular readership.

> Your posts must be accurate, and reflect your own opinions. Even so, some colleagues and staff will see them as divisive and confrontational. Some may think you have gone behind their backs by posting your comments online and not at the table. Be prepared for the inevitable backlash.

> Maintain a professional style, and respect confidentiality and personnel issues when discussing municipal affairs. Your blog should reflect how you want to be perceived in the community.

> Make it clear that what you write represents your personal comments, and cannot be misconstrued as an official statement, or a collective statement representing your municipality.

> It's better to address issues than individuals if you want to make a critical comment. You have potential legal risks when commenting about others, including defamation and libel. Free speech has responsibilities, not just rights.

➤ What do you have to (or want to) say? If you can't keep a regular flow of useful, interesting content, consider using Facebook and Twitter instead.

➤ How will you measure your success? By number of visitors? Number of comments? Reaction on the street or in the coffee shops? Number of daily or weekly posts? Figure it out first, so you can start keeping track right away.

Most blog packages allow you to add photos to any post, so you can turn any entry into a multimedia presentation. If you really want to go multimedia, consider a podcast or video blog instead of a written one.

Blog packages have numerous social networking options such as Facebook and Twitter links, comments, rating, RSS feeds, and more. Use them – although be careful about trackbacks, often used by spammers. If you don't allow comments, your posts will seem arrogant and standoffish. To control spam content, you can require registration for any outside commenters. Users today understand the need for spam moderation and won't begrudge having to register in order to respond.

The Long and the Short of It

If you have a lot to say, and need space to say it, a blog is a good tool. Municipal issues like planning and budgets often require space to explain and to post many images. Blogs are good for that: they provide the space to get into detailed explanations of issues and why you made your decision on any of them.

A typical blog post runs 250 to 750 words. Longer and you run the risk of losing your readers' interest. A really long piece is probably best broken into separate posts or saved as a downloadable PDF with the post only being a summary of the PDF's contents. Make no more than three key points – one of which is the prime focus of your post. You want people to read it all and come away feeling their time was worth the effort.

Social media sites that encourage shorter posts are sometimes referred to as "micro-blogging" sites or "conversational media" sites. Generally, these entries are less formal, shorter (often 200 to 250 characters), and more conversational than a regular blog. As a result, such posts are often of the "here's what I'm doing now" nature. A host of tools and sites offer enhanced micro-blogging options separate from the popular blogging platforms. Twitter has also been described as micro-blogging; however, while Twitter's model stresses micro-content, the delivery method does not fit the blogging model.

If you want to share short bursts of information, updates, a few images, and some links, then a micro-blogging site or Facebook will be easier to keep current and regular. Short posts are also much less time consuming. Twitter is better for the "brief thought of the moment" post. Most likely, if you blog, you will also use Facebook, Twitter, or Google+ to post additional content and links that direct readers to your longer blog posts.

Blogs are important enough that Google has a separate blog search option on its main search engine page (in the "more" menu). This looks for search terms only within the blogosphere. As a politician, you should use it to look for references to yourself and your municipality, not just search through websites.

Good for You, Good for Your Community

Blogging can be good for your political career. If you do it well, maintain reader interest, and keep your blog up to date, you can become a respected voice in your community – and your blog a site where people go for credible views and news. You may even be perceived as a local expert by outsiders. You will become an "influencer" in the social stream. In *Content Nation*, John Blossom wrote, "Through social media, anyone's politics could become everyone's politics."

Most of all, blogging can be good for your community, because you can keep your fellow citizens better informed about both you and the decision-making process you follow.

Chapter 12

Municipalities and Social Media Use

Chris Anderson, editor-in chief of *Wired* magazine, wrote, "Your brand is not what you say it is ... it's what Google says it is." That's somewhat simplistic. It's true that many users find out about products and brands through search engines, and also true that the links on the first page are the most likely to be clicked. But, users talk about products and their choices on social media, and all of their followers and friends get to read their comments. Studies show peer recommendations and comments have a greater impact on buying decisions than advertising.

Anderson says this change has led to the "tyranny of the customer." Although this is another oversimplification, he is right that the customer now has a much louder voice in commenting on brands than with traditional advertising. At the same time, expectations for customer service have risen. Customers expect companies to participate online, to listen to their concerns, and to respond to them. How customers perceive a company or its brand will affect their buying behaviour.

Companies are paying close attention and turning to social media as a tool for improving customer service. Delta Airlines, for example, has 10 staff members who deal with customer service issues 24/7 via a Twitter channel.

Meeting Citizens' Expectations

Municipalities are in the business of delivering customer service, too. Our customers are the residents and ratepayers in our community. Municipalities cannot ignore the trends, or the heightened expectations of our customers. Your municipality is its own brand. It needs to have recognition online and needs to participate actively in the conversations, too.

Municipalities are not structured for social media, however. They must learn how to have a different type of conversation with citizens; not over a counter, not in a controlled office environment, not one-on-one with a single party, and not via a monologue or a slideshow presentation. Municipalities must learn to respond rapidly in accordance with consumer expectations about online communications. They must learn to share. They must learn to trust the community – but also give reasons for the community to trust the government in return.

Be sincere, helpful, open, honest, and share. This builds trust.

To establish that trust, make sure your municipality is never silent when it receives a message, query, comment, or compliment on social media. Acknowledge the messenger. This is a well-tested rule for good customer service. Even if you don't have an immediate answer, say thanks and promise to get back as soon as you have one. Just make sure someone follows up.

Reply like a human, not like one of those despised automated telephone answering systems. Social media is about people-to-people conversations.

Never be afraid to ask your online community for ideas and best practices about running the municipality. Ask what the community thinks about issues and ideas. Take the old-fashioned suggestion box out of the office and put it on social media.

This widespread shift to e-government ("Government 2.0") and cyber-democracy has a learning curve for municipalities. Old ideas about roles, proprietary data, and controlling information are outdated. The new models are collaboration, sharing, creativity, and trust.

Why not make all of your hoarded data open and free, like Vancouver, Toronto, Ottawa, Edmonton, and others have already done? Trust the community to not only use your data wisely, but also to find unexpectedly creative uses, so everyone benefits. (See <data.vancouver.ca> for more on the open data project.)

Social media is tough to fit into spreadsheets and ROI calculations: it doesn't fit comfortably into budgets. It won't return a dividend, a tangible asset, or even a quantifiable result. It's a service and a tool, and it works across departmental boundaries. Companies outside your control hold the reins of power, everyone can have a say, and user interactions can be challenging and stressful. But, it's something you have to join.

Before you decide to participate online, you should have a formal municipal communication policy in place. I discuss this at length in my previous book, *Politically Speaking: Media Relations & Communication Strategies for Municipal Politicians* (Municipal World, 2012) It is important for every municipality to have a clear, written communication policy that outlines the hierarchy of who speaks for what and when. Social media, however, requires a separate section identifying your organization's online policy. For more on creating a social media policy, see Chapter 13.

Next step: go online and look at what others have done – municipalities and other orders of government, private businesses, corporations, and individuals. Look on social media sites to see if neighbouring towns, local industries, and community organizations have a presence. You will want to link to most of these when you establish your own page, and get a link from them in return. Connections like these matter online.

What to Expect from Social Media

Can social media help a community? That's not a yes or no question. It depends on what you expect to get from your effort, and it depends equally on what you put into it. There is no silver bullet answer. Networking on any level is, generally, a good thing. However, read Chapter 4 on what social media is not, and Chapter 6 about results, and compare these ideas with your own perceptions of what social media can do.

Social media can help you monitor many things in your community, including public reaction to issues and announcements, emergencies, local resources, local businesses and the economy, comments on news and events, and even crime. But, to take full advantage of that potential, you need to commit staff resources to monitor and participate in the networks.

In Chapter 4, I compared social media to a garden that needed constant care. It's a complex ecosystem, a mixture of wild and cultivated systems that grow, change, and evolve, sometimes outside our control. And, they often intermingle.

As I explain in Chapter 6, you can expect four outcomes from any media interaction, including social media: information, action (or response), engagement, and influence. You will probably look for a combination of these from your participation.

The organizers of the recent "Occupy Wall Street" movement successfully engaged supporters worldwide by using social media to create awareness and build momentum. They had the advantage of having an issue that resonated with their audience. You can't expect the same sort of widescale response from a municipal issue, but you *can* get local community reaction.

Your Organizational Presence Online

First, you need a social media presence – at the very least on Facebook. Open an account and create a page (a group is less functional for municipal use). Decide what level of openness you want – fully public or restricted – and set the privacy controls before you post anything. Upload some photos to the page's gallery space (see Appendix D about terms of service). I also recommend establishing Twitter accounts, for department heads to start, and for other staff when your policy is completed.

Beware of departmental silos. While big municipalities may require multiple presences on social media, it's far more effective to keep that number small, and instead allow different departments to have administrative access for a single municipal page. Users will find it preferable to be able to get a single municipal feed, and may learn more from a combined feed.

Will too many municipal voices on social networks sound fractured? Will too few sound authoritarian? Are there people who can speak for more than one department? Are there departments that should be compartmentalized with their own voice? Map out the number of accounts you want to maintain early; a coordinated approach avoids redundancies and posting at cross-purposes.

It's not merely an administrative matter: security also becomes a greater challenge when you have multiple accounts.

You can open a business account on Facebook, but you cannot have a personal account *and* a business account at the same time. Business accounts may be easier to administer, but have reduced functionality for networking. As Facebook explains it, "Business accounts are designed for individuals who only want to use the site to administer pages and their ad campaigns. For this reason, business accounts do not have the same functionality as personal accounts. Business accounts have limited access to information on the site. An individual with a business account can view all the pages and social ads that they have created; however, they will not be able to view the profiles (timelines) of users on the site or other content on the site that does not live on the pages they administer. In addition, business accounts cannot be found in search and cannot send or receive friend requests."

Many of your staff, especially those under the age of 40, will already have a social media presence and profiles on or accounts with several social media sites. It will sometimes be difficult for them to work online under a municipal persona and keep it separate from their private profile.

Assigning Responsibilities and Involving Staff

Given the hours Canadians spend online, expect staff to be on the same sites after hours as they are during work. As I wrote in Chapter 9, it is difficult for them to extricate themselves from their work if they are linked to municipal pages or content through personal profiles. You will need a good social media policy to help define roles and responsibilities, and what is expected of them.

Because it's fairly new, there's a natural tendency to assume that social media is the domain of a younger employee, and that older employees are "out of the loop" when it comes to technology and the internet. However, computer use is ubiquitous in the workplace; and, even if everyone is not current with the latest trend or software, this doesn't mean they are not capable of learning and using it. In fact, the largest growth area in the social networking demographics is the 55-years and up group.

When assigning staff to social media tasks, avoid selecting people simply by age. Social media is about people, not simply about the technology. You can train people to use the machinery, but training them to be good in customer relations is much harder. ·

What you want are people who have good interpersonal skills, can work with others, can multitask, have good linguistic skills, and are passionate about their municipality. You want people who don't get offended easily, who can defuse awkward or confrontational situations, and who don't take everything personally.

Ideally, that would also be part of the personality of every politician. Since it's *not*, however, it's best for politicians not to get involved in the municipality's social networking, but let staff do the monitoring and posting. Politicians can create their own individual profiles and pages for themselves. In fact, I encourage them to do so in Chapter 11. But, they should not meddle in what staff is doing or politicize it.

If you see staff doing something that is clearly inappropriate or offensive, or that runs counter to what you believe is council's will, then bring it up through the proper channels within your municipality; but, don't micro-manage the staff over their social media use.

Instead of telling your staff what to do with social media, get them together and ask them to suggest ideas about how to use it. Focus on the benefits and positives of social media use, not on any negative potential.

Can municipal employees access social networks at work? Many municipalities (and private companies) block traffic from sites like Facebook because they feel these distract from the job. A survey from Insites Consulting found a third of all users couldn't access social media from their workplace. Yet, only a quarter of businesses had a written policy about social media use and only a small percentage of employers provided any sort of social media training.

Rather than restrict usage over concerns about possible misuse – which in turn may restrict employees from using social media creatively and for the good of the municipality – hold workshops to guide employees in the behaviour you expect. Reiterate your organization's ethical standards. Unblock social media sites, then gently monitor the traffic and workflow to see what happens. Staff may enjoy being able to check their favourite sites during breaks or lunch, and in turn be happier and more enthusiastic about their jobs.

Building Partnerships and Developing Content

Work with related agencies and associations so they can link to your municipal feed. Your downtown business association, regional tourist association, or chamber of commerce, for example, are good partners. Share their events and activities along with yours. If these organizations are already using social media, networking with them will help bring your new presence to their members.

Post a link to your own media releases and municipal documents on your social network pages, but also consider posting links to your strategic partners' releases. Tweet the links, too.

Citizens can create "fan" pages, groups or "clubs" that relate to your municipality. Sometimes, there can be confusion among users about which is the "official" site, especially if user-created pages have more fans or members than official pages. Look for such pages online and join them so your municipality can be part of the conversations there as well. You may find that many non-permanent or part-time residents are members of these pages, and this gives you a new way to reach them.

Do you tape and broadcast your council meetings? If so, get them on YouTube. When the minutes of the meeting come out, insert the times from the video when that discussion began. More and more Canadians are getting their video and TV shows online. If your council is limited to broadcasting meetings on local cable TV, your audience is evaporating. Put your council on YouTube and you open up a whole new audience. You may reach a generation that is not politically engaged in municipal politics at present.

Use social networks to promote volunteerism, too, by creating a buzz about local volunteer projects. Build the excitement online. A small brush fire online can become a raging forest fire in the real world.

Find out what other municipalities are doing. Speak with their staff about how they implemented their social networking programs, what tools they chose, and how they're managed internally. Don't be afraid to copy the best ideas and practices for your own municipality. Provincial or federal municipal organizations may also be able to help by providing workshops or documents to help get you started.

Taking It to the Next Level

After you have your social media presence established, it's time to reconsider your static website. Can it be upgraded with social media links and features? Can it be simplified and refocused? Does it meet the community's changing needs? Can the community communicate easily with staff and politicians via the website? Can elected officials comment and reach out to the ratepayers through it?

Both Calgary and Nanaimo rebuilt their websites in 2010 to highlight a clean, uncluttered, and user-friendly interface and prominent search box. Both cities put their social media links up front. Nanaimo's are big, bold, colourful, and easy to find.

"Think globally, tweet locally" was the slogan of a presentation about Kitchener's social media experience for the Association of Municipalities of Ontario (AMO) conference in 2010, available as a PDF from the AMO website. Presenters Michael May and Saj Jamal wrote, "It's not a fad. It's a shift in the way we communicate." Kitchener is just one of the many Canadian municipalities that have enthusiastically adopted social media as one of their tools for communication.

In 2009, 20 of Ontario's 444 municipalities had a social media presence. By the end of 2010, that had grown to 125. By now, I expect that number will have more than doubled. Across Canada, the picture is similar: municipalities are getting connected and reaching out through social media. Is your municipality among them?

If your municipality isn't using social media, you're missing an extraordinary opportunity to communicate with your citizens. In his book *Six Pixels of Separation*, author Mitch Joel wrote, "When it comes to the balance between online communications and using social media channels, and whether or not to use your traditional, tried and true communications methods ... social media isn't an 'instead-of.' It's an 'in addition to.'"

The benefits of using social media outweigh the risks.

Chapter 13

Crafting Your Social Media Policy

If your municipality already has a communications policy, especially one with an internet use section, then developing a social media policy won't be as much of a challenge. The basic groundwork will already be in place. However, special aspects of social media should be taken into account. Plus, this policy statement can form the basis of a training guide for all staff.

Social media requires more monitoring than a static website. It requires staff to check several sites regularly (at least daily), post new material, and answer or pass along any questions or concerns that other users have posted in response or on your "wall."

Things to Consider

Here are some things to consider when developing your own policy:

➤ Do you require managerial or administrative approval to post on a social media site or to make a tweet? Or, will you trust staff to post appropriately? If not, how long is the turnaround time between proposed post and approval? Users have expectations about timely responses.

➤ Does administration expect to see all the comments and posts from your wall, or all the tweets directed at your accounts? If so, how often and when? And, how is it distributed?

➤ Is it appropriate for members of council or staff to tweet during a meeting? Post on a social media site? Or to send email?

➤ Do you ask your council and staff to turn off their smartphones at the beginning of a meeting? To hand them over and shut down laptops before entering a closed meeting?

➤ A social media policy not only has to define who does what and when; it has to lay down ethical guidelines. Have you explained what online behaviour is expected of everyone?

➤ Are employees allowed to use pseudonyms or aliases? If so, under what circumstances? When should staff disclose their identities online? Can they comment anonymously on municipally-related topics?

➤ If staff post after work hours on municipal pages or on any social media that might associate them with the municipality, must they disclose this to anyone? If so, when and to whom?

➤ Do staff or members of council have their own blogs, Facebook pages, or other private sites online? If so, have they disclosed their relationship with the municipality? Posting comments that neither reflect nor criticize the relationship should need no disclosure.

➤ Do all posts and comments comply with federal, provincial, and municipal laws, including copyright, defamation, and confidentiality?

➤ How does the municipality respond to a negative or critical comment? How is that comment reported? Who responds?

➤ If a resident posts a question about facilities, services, or other municipal business, who responds to it, and when?

➤ Does your social media policy dovetail with your existing privacy and confidentiality policy?

➤ Is there a process in place for informing police or other authorities if a post appears threatening? Who reports it?

➤ If a mistake is made in a post or comment, who corrects it, when, and how?

➤ Are all employees trained in social media use or just the ones assigned to work with it? Do all staff get copies of your social media policy?

➤ Is social media literacy considered in HR procedures when hiring?

➤ Do the persons assigned the task of managing social media and posting have the necessary language skills? Whatever they post will reflect on the entire municipality.

➤ Does your IT department have a say when determining social media use and policies? (And, if not, why?)

➤ Are all staff computers equipped with a spellchecker that can parse comments and posts on social media and blogs?

➤ Is your municipal calendar of public events also duplicated on your social media calendar? If so, who updates it and how often?

➤ How will you manage and measure your online connections? Will you store user names and pages offline? Who will keep track of the changing number of followers, likes, friends, etc.?

➤ Are staff expected or required to monitor and post on social media outside the office or outside working hours? If so, are they compensated for that work and how? Can they post after hours under their municipal identity, or only under their personal identity? If personal, can they comment on municipal issues? Do they need a disclaimer stating they are not speaking for the municipality?

➤ Do you have municipal partners – charities, service clubs, humane society, or other agencies – that also have Facebook and other social media pages? If so, are they linked (friends or liked) with your municipal accounts?

➤ Do staff have scheduled times for checking social networks or can they check it whenever they wish? What happens when staff get too busy to check?

➤ Will municipal pages have multiple administrators, so that other users can take over if the main user is ill or leaves the job?

➤ Are municipal pages registered under employees' municipal email addresses or personal email addresses?

➤ Can all staff individually subscribe to electronic newsletters or newsfeed services? Or, are these assigned to specific people who distribute them to other staff or politicians as appropriate?

➤ Are some social media services to be used for information only? If so, which and by whom? An example might be using a specific Twitter account for citizens to report problems on local roads, such as potholes or a traffic accident. Conversely, the works department may use that account to broadcast road closures, repairs, and delays. This doesn't need to become a conversational channel, just an information source.

➤ Do all staff and council members use a consistent email signature? Or, are they allowed to create their own unique or departmental signature?

➤ How should staff deal with online harassment? All users are vulnerable to harassment, cyber-stalking, and cyber-bullying. Is someone in your municipality known for writing angry letters to the paper, or calling councillors at all hours to complain about something? Do they come to the municipal office and argue vehemently with staff over minor issues? They may be online, too.

Flag sensitive topics for staff that require higher-level clarification before commenting. These include anything to do with personnel, legal matters, health and safety (such as water quality), and any political matter. Identify these areas so that, when staff on social networks encounter them, they know to bring them to managers or department heads, rather than just wading in with a response.

Will you need to develop a record-keeping system to track online use and time spent on social networks? You might think you need something to measure your investment in social media, but staff might also see it as too controlling and resent having to fill out forms to log their time.

Related Policy Areas

While not specifically about social media, your policy should also clearly state what is and is not appropriate online use of municipally-owned computers. Many municipalities provide laptops for councillors and senior staff that can be taken home and used offsite. Make it clear what is expected of those users: they should not visit sites with pornography, for example, and should avoid sites that promote racial, religious, or gender hatred. Can these laptop users log into personal social media accounts and post on personal blogs? If not, why not?

Add that they should use their home email for personal conversations and the municipal email for any business or interaction related to the municipality. Municipal email is subject to freedom of information legislation and a request to get a copy of it may be filed by anyone. Your communication policy should clearly state that municipal email is not confidential or private except under limited circumstances.

How do you use email signatures? For contact information, your mission statement, or your logo? Are they designed to work equally in HTML and text-only messages?

Do you want to include confidentiality disclaimers? Consult your legal staff about whether such disclaimers have any legal merit. Lengthy disclaimers threatening legal action if the email is shared may be seen as hostile and overly bureaucratic by recipients, especially when the subject matter in the email is clearly not confidential. If you feel you need a disclaimer, consider something brief and neutrally-worded, shorn of the threats.

Craft an agreement for everyone to sign that says they agree that the users, and not the municipality, are responsible for any legal actions that stem from their violation of your policy.

Your policy document won't be carved in stone. It will be subject to change and revision as you learn more about how to best manage your social networking assets. Plan to review it annually, at the very least, to make sure it's up to date with all the sites and services you use.

A simple tool to help you develop a social media policy is found at <policytool.net>. It can lay the groundwork for a more comprehensive policy.

Chapter 14

Influence, Engagement and Counting Friends

Who are the "influencers" in social media? Key people in any social network shift; their influence waxes and wanes. Conversations on social media are not usually included in search engine results, so you may not find them through this method. How do you reach these influencers? How do you become one?

Determining Influence

"Going viral" is a term used since 2006 to describe what happens when a video, email, or post becomes unexpectedly and ragingly popular, being viewed or shared worldwide. No one can say what makes any particular piece of content catch fire, and seize the audience like this.

Is this influence? It can be if the content encourages either action or engagement, and if that call is acted upon. A similar term, "buzz," is also used to describe hot topics that get high viewing or sharing scores; but viral means it spreads uncontrollably, more than just buzzes.

Online, publicity is driven by the public, a radical change in distribution from pre-internet days, when publicity was driven by marketing and advertising agencies or departments. This has changed the way many companies do their marketing online, as they look for ways to get the public to spread the word for them through "viral marketing." Although it's not the same as a video "going viral," it does work on the same principle.

Charlie Sheen and several other celebrities have more than a million followers on Twitter or friends on Facebook. Are they more influential than you? Possibly; but, influence is not measured solely in numbers. Some of those followers are on the bandwagon because everyone else seemed to be joining. Others wanted to see what all the hype was about. Some are there because it's their job to monitor what celebrities do. Some are nosy. Others like to share the patina that comes with being accepted as a "friend" by someone with star quality. There are as many reasons for adding your name to the list as there are followers.

If Charlie Sheen tells his followers to go out and buy red socks, how many will actually do so? What are the limits of his influence? How can it be measured? Celebrities certainly have a greater presence online than you or I; still, they may not have any more influence. In our local circles, we probably have a much greater social media influence.

Douglas Crets, blogger at <Fastcompany.com> calls influencers "the social media tribespeople, who have intimate knowledge of their trade and their profession, but who are not celebrities." These are the people who shape our discussions; buying habits; and political, social, and religious views, yet are not among the glitterati.

"These influencers don't get eight minutes with David Letterman," adds Crets. "They don't get paid handsome bags of lucre a week to tell companies what to do. And, they mean virtually nothing to everyone. They are the information-seeking missiles that every company or brand would be dying to have in their C-suite for five minutes. And, search engines, brands, and executives want to find them. Without them, people are missing out on huge opportunities to solve problems and make money."

Influencers are people we want in our friends list, groups, and circles, and whose tweets we want to follow. Their words carry more weight than the sputterings of the celebrities-du-jour. You may unfriend and unfollow Lady Gaga and her ilk after the novelty wears off, but you will probably keep following the real influencers, the people whose words you heed, whose posts have some depth and value, in your list.

According to a study by Marketing Sherpa, 87 percent of consumers trust a friend's recommendation over a review by a critic. Jupiter Research found social network users are three times more likely to trust a peer opinion than advertising claims when making a purchase decision. These show that influence is not spread from the top down, but rather horizontally across peer networks. You and I can influence our peers as much or more than Charlie Sheen in some areas.

Beyond Friends and Followers

Your online footprint is much more than just friends and followers. How often you contribute to social media (tweet and post), how often you are mentioned, and how often your content is re-posted or forwarded are some of the other metrics that measure influence. Many programs and browser add-ons keep track of these and other data. Klout, for example, is simple and effective, but it measures only Twitter and Facebook. Others include Twentyfeet, Crowdbooster, Tweetstats, Twitalyzer, SocialMention, and MyWebCareer.

You can count the number of visitors to your blog site through built-in metrics, or by using Google Analytics. You can count the number of fans on your Facebook page through the administration panel tools. YouTube has metrics to show the number of views and subscribers, and other tools allow you to track the number of "likes" for every Facebook post, or votes on other social network sites. These numbers have weight when measuring influence.

Traffic doesn't equal community or engagement, however. Sometimes, it's just digital rubbernecking. People may be following you because you're a celebrity. Or maybe because you're so egregiously stupid that they are entertained by you. People are attracted to our mistakes and *faux pas*. When Toronto Mayor Rob Ford allegedly had a screaming fit at the 911 operators in late 2011, it generated a tidal wave of tweets. The event created a lot of traffic about him, little to none of it positive. That traffic wasn't Ford's "community."

There are a variety of apps that will give you a better, deeper overview of your online communities and statistics. These apps can prove to be invaluable tools when trying to estimate your online influence.

Metrics Don't Tell the Whole Story

Measuring your municipality's influence can almost be a full-time job; ultimately, though, the results may not reflect what's happening in your own community. The metrics represent a particular snapshot of activity at a given moment, not your overall presence. What they don't tell you – about a person who read a post or tweet and agreed, or acted upon it outside the internet, or a person who visited your website outside the social media site and not by a click-through – is equally important.

Having fans or followers is not as important as having active members. If you have 25,000 fans on your Facebook page, you may feel successful; but, if only 100 of them actively post or reply, your actual influence is much lower than the apparent fan count. To boost their activity, *you* must participate more. Pay attention to those active members and engage them as often as you can. They are keeping your community alive.

The only thing pundits seem to agree on is that influence grows with online participation. Strive for a positive online influence through your activity, but don't base your model for success solely on the numbers that result from the analyzers.

In the future, search engines will identify not only the content from a website, but also the social network influencers who are posting about it, linking to it, and shifting the public consciousness in some way. To get ranked highly in the search engine of the future, your participation in social media will play an important role.

Chapter 15

A Tool for Marketing and Promotion

Marketing and promotion through traditional methods can be very expensive. Social media offers an inexpensive way to expand your potential market with a modest investment in resources and staff.

How many readers see and respond to an ad in the local newspaper? The average Twitter user has 350 followers. Six percent of tweets get retweeted, so your first tweet reaches 350, the retweet another 7,350. And, if that gets retweeted again by six percent of them, it reaches another 154,350 people (more than 160,000, total audience). The average Facebook user has 130 friends (some sources suggest more). If six percent of friends share a post, it reaches 2,730 more users, and the third time 57,330 (more than 60,000, total). Can you get this sort of audience from an advertisement? And, how much did it cost to run that ad?

It's a noisy world out there with everyone and every municipality vying for attention. Unless yours is a big urban centre, Canadian municipalities are niche markets compared with the big corporations and brands. That doesn't mean it's not worth the effort, though. Still, while you *can* strengthen your niche through social marketing, don't overestimate what you can get from participation.

Successful companies have monetized social media, creating brand loyalties, and using Twitter and Facebook to advertise and promote both brands and specific products. By putting a human face on the companies, providing easy resources for feedback and comment, and giving customer support and service through social media, these companies have built their brands, and established their presence online in ways that would be difficult and expensive to do in the real world. There's no reason municipalities can't follow their example.

Tapping the Opportunities

A lot of untapped opportunities for marketing and promotion lie outside Twitter, Facebook and Google+. All it takes to exploit them is a little imagination and a small risk. For example, does your community host any major festivals or events? Why not offer a limited number of tickets on eBay? Perhaps you can offer only premium tickets that way, and make it a bidding war for them. After all, the audience on eBay is much, much larger than the audience for any municipal website. Advertise the tickets through a link on Twitter and Facebook, too.

Online vendors like eBay do take a small fee for the service of selling your products; but, how much would a ticket agency charge for the same service? And, all such efforts do help put your municipality's name out there.

As another example, Google has a service for context-sensitive advertising – placing small ads on websites in a small box (powered by a script you can't see). When you go to that site, you see text-based ads that relate either to the content on the page itself or to the keywords you entered in a search engine to get to the site. Facebook offers a similar service as well. These services aren't social networking, but rather examples of how context can be used to focus marketing efforts. And, you can use these services to promote your community or your own political career.

Many social networking sites also have a simple poll or survey feature that you can use to measure community reaction to issues or events. Keep your surveys short and easy, and for specific topics, not general ones.

Let Purpose Define Your Strategy

Don't post too often on your corporate wall if you're trying to push something. Users quickly get tired of seeing promotional or obvious marketing posts. Marketing firm Exact Target found 55 percent of Facebook users liked a brand and then later decided they no longer wanted to see the company's posts. The study also showed that half of the fans don't visit the company's page or website after the initial "like." Many only "liked" the company to take advantage of an offer and, when that company failed to offer more special offers, the user "unliked" them.

What are municipalities trying to market? Themselves, of course; but, it's not a product you can put in a box and ship away. You're marketing your friendly businesses, cozy streetscapes, beautiful downtown, and exciting lifestyle. That's where social media comes in: use it to keep people informed in a casual, conversational way about what it's like to live in your community. Use the photo gallery to share pictures of autumn leaves, or images of people skiing, fishing, and hiking. Show off your downtown, your farmers' market, your parks. Do it as any individual would – passionately, enthusiastically, but without the hard sell.

It helps if someone enthusiastic and chatty makes these posts. Their passion will help sell the message to others, and help keep them engaged. Studies of social network use have found positive experiences create bigger conversations than negative ones.

Make video tours of your community. Put them on YouTube, then link them on Facebook or other sites. YouTube is a great resource for promotion. Post links to media stories about your community and region in your networks. Tweet about events and local activities. Social media marketing is a stream, not a series of single events.

Create a community wiki to collect stories and photos from long-time residents. Ask people to write their stories or record them, and have them transcribed. Get local schools and libraries involved. A site showing pride in your heritage would be both a community resource and a marketing tool to attract visitors.

Have your staff create blogs about their strategic issues, such as urban design, recreational facilities and services, waterfront development, the downtown, and similar issues or locations. These don't have to be extensive posts, and will benefit from photos or videos. They will help keep the public informed about these topics on an ongoing basis, not merely when you bring them to the council table.

Chapter 16

E-media and Traditional Media

The proliferation of social media has given rise to a new type of reporter: the citizen journalist – also called "participatory journalists," "e-media," and the "we media."

Thousands of people with no previous experience in the media have become online reporters, broadcasters, and commentators, most learning their trade as they practise it. Blogs, podcasts, and video are their main vehicles of expression. Most of these people post not for profit, but for the satisfaction; but, some do it to further political, social, or religious agendas.

Growing Field, Evolving Tools

This new cadre of amateur journalists have already posted about any and everything, from sports to chess, politics to religion, fishing to grammar. They post on their own schedule. They may write about what they had for breakfast, or make a podcast about the hardware required to get humans to the moon again. Some work for themselves; others for organizations or online media. There are no limits on their reach.

Some are very good: literate, educated, witty, urbane, insightful. Others are dull, clumsy, and inarticulate. Bloggers and podcasters represent a fair cross-section of humanity in their mix of skills and talents. A lot of e-media people have earned solid reputations as writers of quality. Some (like me) are former journalists who moved from traditional to online media. Many have become influencers in the social networks. What they usually lack is the employee relationship with traditional media.

Media "futurists" have predicted that, within a decade, "citizens will produce 50 percent of the news peer-to-peer." One can only hope that, in the interim, the level of grammar and spelling improves in parallel with this trend. As the world saw with the capture and death of Libyan leader Muammar Gaddafi, it doesn't take a formal media crew to capture and distribute breaking news. All it takes is a smartphone and a link to YouTube. You don't even have to do it well to get a worldwide audience.

In a positive development, citizen journalists have recently been given a new tool to boost their presentation quality: AOL's Editors' Room, an online tool that provides videos you can embed into your blog or website. It has a library of clips you can search and, with a few simple clicks, embed them into the site. While the site does not have the rich library that YouTube offers, it is better organized and categorized. That bodes well for improved quality on e-media sites and more professional-style citizen broadcasting.

Dealing with Requests

What should you do if you get a request for an interview or for a comment from one of these e-media journalists?

First, decide for yourself if the person is credible. If they have a relationship with existing traditional media, such as a newspaper or station, even as a freelancer, they likely have credentials you will recognize. Many won't because they are independent. Look at their body of work and determine how to proceed.

Have they blogged about politics or municipal issues in the past? Do they represent a special interest group or ratepayers' organization? Do they have a reputation with municipal staff or a municipal organization? Do they check content to be sure its factual and correct? Do they allow comments on their posts?

What if you get a request for passes to an event or to interview staff? Is there anything in their past work to suggest they will cover that event online as would any traditional media?

It will be up to you to check the e-media person's blog, tweets, or Facebook page to determine if you feel he or she has credibility, or if you want your comments posted on their site or your interview broadcast in their podcast. Take the request seriously and, if at all possible, grant it.

Treat the e-media with the same respect you treat traditional media. It's another issue of trust.

Many people enter the media, even the e-media, for the same reasons politicians choose to enter public service: to make a change for the better, to contribute, to improve, to accomplish things for the community, and to protect the public interest. E-media, however, is easier to enter than traditional media because (like politics) there is no requirement for talent, education, or experience. Media is the lens through which the public sees politics and politicians. Most people can't sit in council chambers or legislatures and watch the ongoing debates. We depend on someone to tell us what happened and why. Since they were present and we weren't, we respect their opinion on how events unfolded.

Building E-media Relationships

The public perceives media as a public service, even though we all understand intellectually that media is independent and private business. Emotionally, we feel it belongs to us. That feeling is heightened by the internet, because e-media is driven by home-based citizen journalists more than traditional ones who work for those private businesses. We forgive citizen journalists their mistakes more leniently than we forgive mistakes in traditional media because we see them as one of us.

Citizen journalists may not be trained in libel and defamation laws, and may not respect your confidentiality the same way traditional journalists might. They may not check facts very diligently. Even when you trust them, do not say anything "off the record" or repeat confidential information to them. They work outside the normal oversight, structure, and peer pressures that exist in traditional media. As with all journalists, be careful what you say to or do with them, but do try to engage them.

And, as with any reporter, don't argue with e-media online. Not only will it be a very public spat that stains your reputation, but it's one you can never win. Mark Twain said, "Never argue with someone who buys ink by the barrel and paper by the ton." In the same vein, never argue with someone who has a broadband connection, a keyboard, a blog, and infinite time on his or her hands. You can debate, of course; just be careful not to cross the line and let it become vituperative or personal.

I suggested in Chapter 10 that you contact local bloggers and e-media people to get them into your network. Send them invitations to like your pages or to befriend them. Get them involved and make them part of your network. Even when you disagree, they will be helping disseminate your name when they comment. Getting them into municipal social networks means they are more likely to publish content about municipal events and issues to which they are connected.

Chapter 17

Afterword

Every 60 seconds there are more than 695,000 Facebook status updates, 168 million emails are sent, 600 new videos are uploaded to YouTube, 98,000 tweets are sent, 1,500 posts are made on blogs, 6,600 pictures are uploaded to Flickr, and 100 new LinkedIn accounts are opened. By the time this book is published, those statistics will have gone up.

For politicians and the municipalities they serve, getting involved with social networking is not only inevitable, it's a natural extension of what they do. You can't stay outside and not participate any more than you can refuse to have a phone. Remember when faxes first arrived? Everyone was skeptical of them; then, suddenly, they were everywhere and we wondered how we ever conducted business without them.

Social media is now to communications what the fax was a couple of generations ago. Faxes were like Web 1.0: one-way communication, a monologue. It's time to step up into two-way conversations with social media and Web 2.0.

If you're new to social networking online, then proceed slowly, but not at a glacial speed. Plan on being involved within, say, 30 or 60 days after you decide to participate. Spend that time taking a look at your options, seeing what others have done, talking to other politicians or municipalities, and discussing strategies with staff. Decide which steps to take first and learn what you need to do to get started. Read the experiences of other municipalities and learn from them (Kitchener has a great, downloadable report on their website, in PDF format).

In that time, develop your own municipal policy for social media use. At the very least, write down the outline of a policy to complete later, when you have a little more experience online.

After that, all it needs is commitment and some enthusiasm. Like learning to swim, it won't be long before it feels natural. Don't worry, you'll do just fine; the water is warm and not too deep.

~~~~~

In my previous book, *Politically Speaking: Media Relations & Communication Strategies for Municipal Politicians* (Municipal World, 2012), I provided a bibliography for further reading. The irony in offering a book list about online material is not lost on me, even though I quote from several excellent titles. For more information, use your favourite search engine. It's all there, online. Search and read.

Appendix A

CMS: Content Management Systems

A Content Management System (CMS) uses a database manager to provide content to the user's screen, working through templates to manage the design of the display. Some CMSs were developed specifically to create social networks; others have add-in social networking features and connect with social media sites.

Many municipal websites run on a CMS platform (Drupal, Joomla, and Wordpress are the most popular free packages). These platforms can integrate and work with existing social media, but are not designed to be social networks. They are sophisticated database managers and require separate modules or add-ons to implement additional features: to incorporate posting comments to Facebook or Twitter – or even to establish a municipal forum where residents can post comments and questions. These systems have to be installed and set up before they can be used.

Some CMSs also have an accessory blog package. While not as powerful as a stand-alone blog package, this option could also provide a workspace for municipal politicians to collectively comment and express themselves. For residents, the advantage is having all municipal blogs together in one space. The disadvantage is that the individual writers may not feel they have enough profile in the crowd. This might be alleviated somewhat by having a link to an external blog for those politicians who already have one.

Others might find it difficult to write, and may feel competition from those who write easily. Still, giving everyone the same opportunity should be considered. The naysayers may come around to it later.

One of the advantages of the CMS model is that portions of these packages can be tagged for internal or public use. There can be a staff forum, notice board, or a blog area not visible to the public and accessed via a password. These areas can also be used to notify staff about upcoming events, job vacancies, changes in benefits packages, etc.

A CMS is not the ideal tool for social networking; but, if you're already using one for your municipal website, it makes good sense to incorporate any networking add-ons.

Wordpress, the blogging platform described in Chapter 5, is also a CMS that can be used for website creation, as well as blogs. It is not as rich an environment as Joomla or Drupla, but will suit many users' needs.

There are also commercial CMS platforms that let users create and design their own social networks and online communities, including programs that integrate with Facebook, Twitter, and YouTube, as well as providing stand-alone functions. Such platforms may allow administrators to charge members for services or collect donations, as well as sell ads or even merchandise. Basically, such platforms provide a *toolkit* for creating a community, rather than a community itself.

The monthly fee for hosting on commercial platform servers varies according to the size of the network you intend and the features you want to incorporate. Speak with your IT people to learn more about what your municipality uses and whether it can be enhanced for social media and interaction.

Appendix B

Where Do We Go from Here?

Web 1.0 was known as the "read and distribute" technology, replete with static websites and one-way communication. Social media are the tools of today's Web 2.0: they are participatory and collaborative. So what, then, is Web 3.0?

Is Web 3.0 the semantic web – the place where smart computers understand the data and the content we provide, and start creating and manipulating the data for us? Is it application-based, focused on more graphically capable environments – "non-browser applications and non-computer based devices ... geographic or location-based information retrieval"? Is it Artificial Intelligence? Is it the "re-empowerment" of experts and authorities on the web? Is it new and innovative Web 2.0 services that come with a profitable business model? Is it web with TV-quality open video, 3D simulations, augmented reality, human-constructed semantic standards, and pervasive broadband, wireless, and sensors? Is it peer-to-peer networks, community-driven workflow, common-interest communities, and "cloud" computing? Is it more location-based apps and services?

No one knows. It's a guessing game for the pundits and you can find all of these suggestions – and many more – in an online search. Predictions often fall short of reality, and the actualities can be far more surprising than our best guesses.

And, what about Web 4.0, already being debated by the pundits? How much further can it go?

Companies have a tough choice: do they design applications based on what they predict users will want in three, five, or 10 years? Or, do they build them based on what users want right now? Does creating the application create the demand? By the time today's demands are met, will the apps be stale and outdated? Is a trend just a fad – or is it something crucial to continued success?

These are questions for companies like Google and Facebook. Like any corporation, their ability to react to the market, to change with user demands, and to innovate slows as they grow. The new trends and shapes that make the next generations of web apps will likely be born in smaller enterprises.

One of the trends that may blossom is the collaborative storytelling site. Interactive storytelling lets people share their experiences in a socially supportive environment. It takes the conversations of social media sites to another level. It's a good tool for a "creative community" project: creating a database to preserve your community's oral heritage. Perhaps your library or museum could set it up in conjunction with your other municipal sites.

Another trend beyond mere conversation is towards creative and practical social networking. Sites like <mightybell.com> provide collaborative tutorials, learning, DIY projects, vacations, and life experiences. Municipalities could use these sites to offer self-guided tours through the area, or to walk people through complex planning or building applications. These offerings integrate with existing social media.

Another shift is collaboration between the internet and television. While some traditional media have struggled to be viable in the face of competition from the internet, TV has developed a symbiotic relationship. TV shows (and associated gossip) is one of the hottest topics on social networks. A survey by the Cable and Telecommunications Association for Marketing in late 2011 showed almost half of all Canadians get their TV shows and movies online, rather than through cable or satellite. And, a third of respondents were considering cancelling their TV service entirely.

This trend is much more than just a rehash of standard broadcasting (itself called internet TV). WebTV is a platform for independent broadcasters to create their own media stream. Social TV is the trend to use mobile devices to connect with friends (including via social media) while watching the same TV show in different locations.

Both niche networks (or micro-networks) and aggregators may grow in popularity as users get fatigued by the size and volume of the bigger social media services. Municipal social networks may be comfortably placed as niche networks, especially if they link to the bigger service providers. Other pundits believe users prefer the all-in-one site, and that the bigger players will eat their competition.

Tablet computers are surging in popularity, and becoming more powerful, with more features and options to edge out netbooks as portable internet devices. Widespread use of tablets will further enhance social networking's role in our daily lives. This will drive development of more mobile-specific apps to enhance networking.

You can stay abreast of online developments in hardware, social media, and internet trends by visiting tech websites or subscribing to email newsletters. Google news alerts are handy for getting links to current stories. However, the information flow will be large; and, unless you're technically inclined, it will be rather opaque. Use your IT department resources to keep your municipality on-target and to identify the truly important trends that might impact your ability to effectively communicate with and engage your community. You don't need to implement any technologies simply because they look new and exciting. But, you really should keep an eye on how social media and the web are changing, so you can be prepared to make changes.

Don't confuse the purpose with the technology that facilitates it. "Social media is about sociology and psychology more than technology," said Brian Solis, CEO of FutureWorks. "Social media is pervasive and it is transforming how people find and share information and how they connect and collaborate with one another."

Appendix C

QR Codes and Other Mobile Uses

QR (Quick Response) codes are the natural evolution of the barcode. QR codes have tiny black blocks arranged on a square pattern against a white background. This can hold a remarkable amount of information in a very small space – up to 7,089 numeric characters or 4,296 alphanumeric characters in the very densest version (version 40). More common are the smaller QRs – version 4 holds up to 114 alphanumeric characters, and version 10 holds up to 395.

Typically, a QR code will contain a URL or link to a website. It may contain an email address, name, phone number, or short message.

You need a QR code reader or "scanner" to decipher them. These apps are available for most smartphones and tablets, and work through the device's camera. Point the camera at the code, press the shutter button, and the device retrieves the content. If it's a URL, the device's browser will usually open to that page. It's a good way to direct consumers to more product information, photos, videos, real estate listings, etc.

QR codes relieve the user of having to type lengthy URLs on a tiny keypad. For manufacturers, they're a dream because a lot of information can be put on a website that won't fit on a product tag.

The use of these codes is growing, but has recently faced the challenge of malicious codes being developed. For example, codes may change the permission status on camera functions, even allowing the phone to be used to send data remotely – including personal data stored on the phone. QR codes could direct users to websites that have programming to manipulate your phone and steal your identity. As a basic caution, do not open QR codes found in emails, and make sure you back up all the data on your smartphone regularly.

Several free online QR code generators and even some downloadable versions are available for your computer. QR generation plug-ins may also be available for popular graphics programs.

QR codes are in their infancy, but have great potential for future use on mobile platforms.

Between a quarter and half of all internet users access the internet from a mobile device. Mobile computing on phones has been around for the past decade, but the development of the iPad and other tablet computers has pushed mobile use statistics up. It is predicted mobile devices will be the primary means of internet access by 2020.

Coupled with the improvements in handheld hardware is the tremendous growth of wireless (WiFi) access and mobile data transmission. According to networking giant Cisco, global mobile data traffic grew 2.6-fold in 2010: three times the size of the entire global internet traffic in 2000. The average smartphone data use in 2010 was 79MB per month, up from 35MB in 2009. There were three million tablets connected to the network in 2010; but, each tablet generated five times the traffic of the average smartphone. Cisco predicts a 26-fold increase in mobile data traffic by 2015 and says tablets will generate as much traffic in 2015 as the entire global mobile network did in 2010.

Access through mobile devices has made people even more connected and raised their expectations about interactivity and quick response times. It has also extended social networking by the development of apps that make it easier to post online on a small screen.

The real bottleneck for smartphones remains the tiny virtual or real keyboard. Even the largest smartphone keyboards are miniscule compared to the smallest netbook. Tablet computers like the iPad have improved mobile use by providing a larger space for input. Some tablets even have auxiliary keyboards that make input faster and far more efficient.

The future of mobile computing is still being written, but the trends mark a growing importance. Tablets are becoming more common, and even ebook readers are now coming with built-in internet access. Netbooks have lost sales to tablets as these surge ahead. We're still waiting for an integrated tablet-and-smartphone device, but that can't be too far along.

Appendix D

Copyright, Fair Use, and Intellectual Property

This is too large a topic to do justice to here; and, I am not a lawyer, so my interpretations may be inaccurate. However, it is important to consider a few legal and cultural aspects of copyright.

Copyright essentially means the right to first publish, reproduce, perform, transmit, and show a work in public. In Canada, everything you write and publish, online and offline, is your copyright unless you otherwise assign it (to a book or magazine publisher, for example). That means no one can copy your content wholesale and reuse it without your permission.

Under the notion of "fair use" or "fair dealing," some of your content may be reproduced. Fair use allows other people to use a part of your content in context with their own. If you post a comment about municipal spending in your blog, then the local newspaper can use quotes from it in an article or editorial, but not reproduce the piece in its entirety. Literary critics can quote from a book being reviewed under the "fair use" provision. A film review site may post stills or even a very short video clip from that movie in a review. Fair dealing also lets your content be reproduced for research and study.

The same protection applies for your own videos and photographs: they have your copyright. However, it gets murky when you post content on a site outside Canada where the copyright laws are different. Do you play by your rules or theirs? It gets even more opaque when you post on a site where the user agreement you accepted says that all of the content on their site belongs to the site owners, or at least while they host it. What if this conflicts with Canadian copyright law? Whose rules apply if there is a legal battle? I don't know, but I've lost sleep over it.

Facebook's old user agreement stated, "By posting User Content to any part of the Site, you automatically grant ... an irrevocable, perpetual, non-exclusive, transferable, fully paid, worldwide license ... to use, copy, publicly perform, publicly display ... such User Content for any purpose ..."

In other words, it owned everything you posted, forever. In 2011, that was amended to a more user-friendly, but still restrictive and potentially litigious agreement: You own all of the content and information you post on Facebook, and you can control how it is shared through your privacy and application settings. In addition:

> For content that is covered by intellectual property rights, like photos and videos ("IP content"), you specifically give us the following permission, subject to your privacy and application settings: you grant us a non-exclusive, transferable, sub-licensable, royalty-free, worldwide license to use any IP content that you post on or in connection with Facebook ("IP License"). This IP License ends when you delete your IP content or your account unless your content has been shared with others, and they have not deleted it.

So, now you own it, but as long as Facebook hosts it, the company has all rights to it. That's one reason it's best to put any photos, documents, or videos on a static website you own, then link them on Facebook or other social media, rather than upload it.

YouTube has a very clear statement on ownership in its TOS: "For clarity, you retain all of your ownership rights in your Content. However, by submitting Content to YouTube, you hereby grant YouTube a worldwide, non-exclusive, royalty-free, sublicenseable and transferable license to use, reproduce, distribute, prepare derivative works of, display, and perform the Content in connection with the Service ..." In other words, it's yours, but you assign YouTube the right to use it as they see fit as long as they host it.

On the other hand, Google's Picasa photo sharing site offers this notice: "Google does not claim any ownership in any of the content, including any text, data, information, images, photographs, music, sound, video, or other material, that you upload, transmit or store in your Picasa account. We will not use any of your content for any purpose except to provide you with the Service."

Google's free Gmail service has this statement: "Google does NOT claim ANY ownership in any of the content, including any text, data, information, images, photographs, music, sound, video, or other material, that you upload, transmit or store in your Gmail account. We will NOT use ANY of your content for any purpose except to provide you with the Service."

However, the terms of service for Google+ are far more restrictive:

> By submitting, posting or displaying the content, you give Google a perpetual, irrevocable, worldwide, royalty-free, and non-exclusive license to reproduce, adapt, modify, translate, publish, publicly perform, publicly display, and distribute any Content which you submit, post or display on or through, the Services.

You agree that this license includes a right for Google to make such Content available to other companies, organizations, or individuals with whom Google has relationships for the provision of syndicated services, and to use such Content in connection with the provision of those services.

You understand that Google, in performing the required technical steps to provide the Services to our users, may (a) transmit or distribute your Content over various public networks and in various media; and (b) make such changes to your Content as are necessary to conform and adapt that Content to the technical requirements of connecting networks, devices, services, or media. You agree that this license shall permit Google to take these actions.

For anyone leery of granting a large corporation what seems like open rights over content you post, <unthink.com> offers a more palatable TOS:

> You grant to UNTHINK, its agents and its assigns a limited, royalty-free license to use, modify, display, reproduce, and distribute such content only in the manner you have authorized. You can revoke this limited license at any time by deleting the affected content. Keep in mind that others may have copies of anything you have shared with them.

Are hyperlinks copying or publishing? No. It's possible to use some of another site's content by simply linking to it. If you show an image from another site on yours by linking and not actually copying the content itself, are you violating their copyright? Not according to the legal opinions I've read. Be careful not to overuse this privilege on your blog or home web pages. Linking to content also increases the traffic on the linked site.

What about streaming video and audio? Or YouTube videos? These display content from another site through an app, but the site running the app (yours) doesn't host the content. It's another grey area for copyright, although not in the forefront of any current legal challenges.

Treat anything you post on social media as giving it away, at least until users revolt and refuse to upload until the terms of service are modified to be more customer-centric. If possible, first post your content on a site you own and link to it on the social network, rather than uploading it there. If you can't link it, at least upload it to your own site before you upload it to a social media site to establish precedent.

Because a lot of people treat anything online as "fair game," and use it without attribution or credit – in fact some will simply steal it and publish it under their own name – consider using a Creative Commons licence to indicate your content may be re-used with attribution. The Creative Commons site offers different licences to suit your preferences or needs.

Google's efforts to scan and make available every book in print also challenges our traditional notions of copyright and intellectual property.

Copyright law is complex and often mystifying. Get advice from your legal staff or service, but advice won't protect your content if someone wants to take it and use it without your permission. There's an enormous amount of piracy online. Even the strictest laws can't cope with the complications that services like Torrent and other peer-sharing apps provide. You could use scripts on your website to control copying by the casual user, but tech-aware people know how to get around them.

I can only recommend you do not post or upload anything you do not wish to lose control over. Treat uploaded photos and videos as gifts to the community at large, and don't get upset by any non-commercial re-use of that content. Sharing is a virtue on social media.

And, treat the content of others with the same respect you want for your own: don't use it without getting the owner's approval first.

Appendix E

Glossary of Common Terms

Aggregator: A website or software that brings together specific information from multiple online sources and displays the results on a single page. For example: a news aggregator, a review aggregator, or a social network aggregator. Many aggregators only show a small amount of the content with a link to its source.

Astroturfing: Generating artificial buzz or interest in a product, service, or idea by pretending it comes from the grass roots.

Avatars: Graphic images that represent the user. In virtual worlds, they can be fully 3D. On most sites, they are small, 2D images. Some systems offer a limited choice of avatars; others let you upload your own (i.e., a photograph). Use of avatars may be mandatory or optional, depending on the service.

Back channel: Private communications between individuals, sometimes set up behind websites, away from public access.

Blog: A portmanteau word from "web" and "log" referring to a digital journal, diary, or news report on any topic. Bloggers can be individuals or groups. Content is shown with the newest posts first.

Blogosphere: The whole universe of blogs on the internet, and the conversations taking place within that realm.

Blogroll: A list of related blogging sites displayed within a blog, identifying those the blogger reads or comments on regularly. This may also include links to help files and registration information.

Bookmarking: Saving the URL (address) of a website in your browser's favourites list, or on a social bookmarking site.

Cloud computing: Accessing data from anywhere, rather than being tied to a particular computer. Shared resources, software, and information are provided to users over the internet.

CMS: Content management systems are suites of integrated software tools that can be used to create static webpages, blogs, wikis, photo galleries, database search and retrieve, and other functions.

Creative Commons: A not-for-profit organization and licensing system where creators can define their own level of copyright and the ways others may use their works.

Crowdsourcing: Harnessing the skills and enthusiasm of social network connections to take ownership of issues and interests and pursue them or solve problems associated with them.

Cyberspace: A term coined by cyberpunk author William Gibson, now widely used as a general term for the internet or world wide web.

Ebook: An electronic book that can be downloaded and read on your computer, reader, or other handheld device. PDF documents can be ebooks, but other file formats are also used.

Flash mob: A group contacted through text messages, social media, or viral emails, which gathers on short notice for a specific purpose, takes action, then disperses quickly.

Forums: Discussion areas where members can post messages, comment on existing messages, and usually send private messages to one another. Forum discussions can be managed and facilitated ("moderated") to maintain the style and image the forum wishes to present.

Friends: Contacts who link to you and who you allow to read your updates, tweets, or wall posts. Members must ask to join someone's friend list.

Hashtag: #, also called a number sign. Used to identify searchable keywords in a tweet (i.e., #municipal). When you search a hashtag word, Twitter shows the relevant tweets that used it, not just those you follow. Also used when organizing tweet-ups.

Link bait: Any content or feature in a website designed specifically to gain attention or encourage others to share or link to the website. Often used as a viral marketing tool.

Lurkers: People who read, but don't contribute to, the conversation. Passive monitoring of content.

Moblogging: Short for mobile blogging: posting from a smartphone or tablet.

Newsreader: Website or browser tool that gathers content from blogs, news sources, or other sites with RSS feeds. The feed is presented as one source display, so you don't have to visit several different sites.

Peer-to-peer: Interaction between two users of a network. Each peer is connected to other peers, allowing sharing and interchange through one another. Often used for file sharing and piracy through services like Torrent.

Podcast: An audio or video broadcast similar to a written blog. Some are on YouTube or iTunes; others are streamed through their author's website. Most can be downloaded to watch or listen to offline. Originally intended for iPod use, but are playable on all media players.

Profile: The information about yourself you post in your social media account. This usually includes basic information and contact data, but may also have much richer content about your past, your interests, hobbies, and employment. It may allow a picture and links to your websites. Some profile content can be marked private or restricted to defined groups.

RSS: Really Simple Syndication, a method of content delivery that allows you to subscribe to content on blogs and other social media and have it delivered to you through a feed that has most formatting features stripped away. You can view feeds from RSS-enabled sites by subscribing to an aggregator or newsreader service.

SMO: Social Media Optimization. Generating publicity and interest through social media, rather than through search engines.

Social bookmarking: Sharing favourites or bookmarks, and sometimes content, with other users through a bookmarking website. Shared items can be voted on, and ranked by popularity.

Spam: Unsolicited bulk email or other electronic messages. Can also refer to spam in blogs, wiki spam, online classified ads spam, mobile phone messaging spam, internet forum spam, and social networking spam.

Splogs: Spam blogs. Pseudo-blogs, full of links or content from other sites in order to boost search engine results.

Tags: Freely chosen keywords attached to a blog post, photo, or content to help identify that content and provide additional searchable terms. Less structured than "categories."

Tag cloud: A visual representation of the popularity of the tags in a blog or website, with the most popular tags shown in a larger typeface.

Thread: A strand of conversation, usually on a forum, in which all the responses are related to and grouped with the initial post.

Trackback: A feedback service that allows bloggers to leave a link (a trackback) on a site to a piece they wrote about another blogger's post. Often used by spammers to leave links to junk, scams, and phishing sites.

Troll: A person who comments angrily about something you posted. Trolls usually contradict your opinions aggressively; resort to insult, invective, and personal insult in replies; and flog the same arguments over and over in subsequent posts. They thrive on the attention they get from bad behaviour, so the best remedy is to ignore them and ban them from commenting on your own blog.

Tweet: A text-based post of up to 140 characters sent through Twitter. Often sent via mobile devices.

Tweet-a-thon: A fundraising campaign on Twitter. Users encourage their followers to tweet about and donate to a particular charitable cause over a specified period of time.

Tweet-up: A gathering of people who use Twitter. Users often include a hashtag to publicize a tweet-up.

URL: Uniform Resource Locator: the global address of pages, documents, and other content on the internet. For example, <http://www.mywebsite.com/myblog>.

VOIP: Voice Over Internet Protocol. A system that lets you use the internet for phone calls. Some systems allow calls to be made to other VOIP subscribers without additional charge, including conference calls. Calls may be audio only or full audio-video. It is often used by e-media for podcast interviews. The best-known VOIP tool is Skype.

Web 2.0: Coined by O'Reilly Media in 2004 to describe internet-based services and sites that emphasize collaboration and sharing, rather than simple publishing of static information (Web 1.0).

Wiki: Web pages designed to present information or work that can be edited collaboratively. Wikipedia is an online encyclopedia created by thousands of contributors worldwide.

Viral: Exceptionally popular, off the charts, spreads wildly. No one knows why something becomes viral. It can be a video of a kid dancing with a Star Wars prop, a snippet from late-night TV, an advertisement, a cat trying to fit into a box, a quote by a politician. Something viral captures the public's attention and it gets shared, passed around, and viewed by thousands, even millions of people, in a short time.

Virtual world: An online graphic, 3D environment where you create an avatar to represent you, and socialize with other residents.

Warez: Copyrighted software distributed illegally through an online file-sharing site (unlike commercial software counterfeiting, which is usually done through retail outlets). Copy protection is usually hacked or broken. Warez is frequently infected with one or more viruses.

OTHER MUNICIPAL WORLD PUBLICATIONS

To order any of the following Municipal World publications, contact us at: <mwadmin@municipalworld.com>, 519-633-0031 or 1-888-368-6125, or visit <books.municipalworld.com>.

Cultural Planning for Creative Communities (Hume) – Item 0035

Deputy Returning Officers Handbook – Item 1280

Electing Better Politicians: A Citizen's Guide (Bens) – Item 0068

Guide to Good Municipal Governance (Tindal) – Item 0080

Making a Difference: Cuff's Guide for Municipal Leaders Volume 1: A Survival Guide for Elected Officials (Cuff) – Item 0059-1

Making a Difference: Cuff's Guide for Municipal Leaders Volume 2: The Case for Effective Governance (Cuff) – Item 0059-2

Measuring Up: An Evaluation Toolkit for Local Governments (Bens) – Item 0061

Municipal Election Law – Item 1278

Municipal Ethics Regimes (Levine) – Item 0045

Off the Cuff: A Collection of Writings Volume 1 (Cuff) – Item 0055-1

Off the Cuff: A Collection of Writings Volume 2 (Cuff) – Item 0055-2

Off the Cuff: A Collection of Writings Volume 3 (Cuff) – Item 0055-3

Ontario's Municipal Act – codified consolidation – Item 0010

Ontario's Municipal Conflict of Interest Act: A Handbook (O'Connor/ Rust-D'Eye) – Item 0050

Open Local Government 2 (O'Connor) – Item 0030

Politically Speaking: Media Relations & Communication Strategies for Municipal Politicians (Chadwick) – Item 0075

Procurement: A Practical Guide for Canada's Elected Municipal Leaders (Chamberland) – Item 0070

Public Sector Performance Measurement: Successful Strategies and Tools (Bens) – Item 0060

Rediscovering the Wealth of Places: A Municipal Cultural Planning Handbook for Canadian Communities (Baeker) – Item 0025

Roadmap to Success: Implementing the Strategic Plan (Plant) – Item 0084

Run & Win: A Guide to Succeeding in Municipal Elections (Clarke) – Item 0020

Stepping Up to the Climate Change Challenge (Gardner/Noble) – Item 0095

Strategic Planning for Municipalities: A Users' Guide (Plant) – Item 0085

Taking Back Our Cities (Hume) – Item 0034

The Local Food Revolution (Hume) – Item 0036

Truth Picks: Observations on This Thing Called Life (de Jager) – Item 0090